Also by Suze Orman

You've Earned It, Don't Lose It
The 9 Steps to Financial Freedom

ASK SUZE

SUZE ORMAN'S ANSWERS TO THE FINANCIAL QUESTIONS EVERYONE WANTS TO ASK

SUZE ORMAN

Three Rivers Press
New York

Copyright © 1997 by Suze Orman

Published by Three Rivers Press, a division of Crown Publishers, Inc.,
201 East 50th Street, New York, New York 10022. Member of the
Crown Publishing Group.

Random House, Inc. New York, Toronto, London, Sydney, Auckland

http://www.randomhouse.com/

THREE RIVERS PRESS and colophon are trademarks of Crown
Publishers, Inc.

Printed in the United States of America

Library of Congress Cataloging-in-Publication Data
is available upon request.

ISBN 0-609-80126-0

10 9 8 7 6

To the Reader

Over the past year, hundreds of viewers from QVC have called or written with questions about investments, debts, home mortgages and ownership, wills and trusts (or lack thereof), Medicaid, long-term-care insurance, life insurance, college planning, bankruptcy, saving now for later, and a variety of other topics. I've noticed that the same questions tend to come up again and again. Finally, I thought, why not put all the questions in one place so you can find the answers easily? That's the idea behind this book, Ask Suze. I've taken the most pertinent questions I'm asked most often and answered each one. You can read the book straight through, or if there's just one subject you're concerned about, such as how to qualify for Medicaid, you can turn to that specific section. If there's a particular term that you want to learn about, such as "revocable living trust," you can also look in the index to see the pages where that term comes up. I hope you'll keep this book nearby and use it often as a quick reference guide. And always remember that what I want most is to help you with whatever problem you have right away. If you need information you can't find here, see the last page of this book for how you can contact me personally.

Suze Orman

WILLS AND TRUSTS

There are many areas of our financial lives that we just don't like to deal with. In fact, I know many people who refuse to deal at all with the topic covered in this particular section. How many of you reading this have a will? Not many, hmm? Well, I can tell you with 100 percent certainty that you will definitely need at least a will, and perhaps a trust as well, sometime in the future. The real question is not *if* you will need it but *when*. It is not that hard or complicated to set all your affairs in order—all you have to do is *do it*.

WILLS

Q. What is a will?

A. A will is simply a document that indicates who you want to receive your money and possessions after your death. It can even be a document you write yourself by hand, although all wills have to fulfill certain requirements to be legal.

Q. Is it hard to get a will?

A. No—it is as easy as can be. Most of you can easily go to a lawyer and have one drawn up—this will cost around

$80 to $100. Or you can use a form will, which you can get at a stationery store. Or if you want, you can draw one up yourself, using one of many books available at any bookstore, or with the help of a computer program.

Q. What happens if I do not have a will?

A. You might say that all people have wills, whether they know it or not. That is, if you can't decide or haven't designated who should receive your assets when you die, the decision has been made automatically by the laws of your state.

When you die without a will, the legal term for what happens is *intestate succession*. Each state has its own laws governing this situation. Let's say you live in California, for instance, and you die without a will. You are considered to have died *intestate*. The laws of California state that if you are married and have one child, of everything that you own in your own name, half will go to your spouse and half will go to your child. If you have two children, one-third will go to your spouse and two-thirds to your children. If you are not married and have no children, all your possessions will go to your parents if they are still alive or to your brothers and sisters if your parents are deceased; and if you do not have either, then to your cousins, and so forth. The point is that unless you have a will or other legal document stating differently, how and to whom your possessions will pass has already been decided for you.

Q. Are you saying that if I do not have a will and I die, my brother—who is my only living relative, and whom I do not get along with at all—will get everything that I have?

A. Yes, that is exactly what I am saying. *If you don't put your wishes in a legal document, they are not likely to be honored.* Your brother may like you far better after you are gone than he did when you were alive if you die without having taken care of this.

Q. If I have a will and I want to change my mind about whom I am leaving things to, can I?

A. Absolutely. If a lawyer drew up your will, just call that attorney and he or she will make the changes for you. Lawyers will draft what is called a *codicil* to your will. If you did not use a lawyer to begin with, you could do this yourself as well. If your will is not very complicated, you may find it's just as easy to draw up a whole new will.

Q. If I draw up a new will, do I have to make sure that my old will is destroyed?

A. Yes, that is usually a good idea. But if that is not possible for whatever reason, then you should know that the will with the latest date on it will be the one that is considered the valid will. I recommend that you make sure your loved ones who are supposed to receive your possessions have an updated copy of the latest version of your will.

Q. Does my divorce from my spouse make my will I had drawn up when we were married null and void?

A. *No.* Your will is still going to be in effect after a divorce. So if you don't want your ex-spouse to inherit those goodies from you, it is essential that you change your will immediately to reflect your new wishes.

Q. I am in a second marriage, and I want to make sure that when I die my children get everything that I own. How can I make sure that this happens?

A. The most important thing to know is this: They will get everything you own if you leave it to them via a legal document such as a will—as long as you do not own anything with someone other than them in what is called *joint tenancy with right of survivorship* (JTWROS). JTWROS is just one way you and another person can hold title to your real estate, brokerage accounts, or a variety of other investments. When you hold title this way, you have made the decision that if you were to die, the other person (who has survived you and is on title with you) would automatically have the right to your half of the investment. It would pass immediately to that person regardless of what you designated in your will.

Let's say that you own a home right now that you hold with your spouse from your second marriage in joint tenancy with right of survivorship. You convince your new husband that since the money that you both used to buy this new house originally came from your divorce settlement from your first husband, then if you were to die, it would be only right that your children from that marriage get the money from the house. So you draw up a will that says this house is to go to your children when you die. Watch out! JTWROS overrides the instructions of any will. When you die, your new husband will end up with the house *regardless of what your will says.*

One way to guarantee that your children would get the house is to own the home in your own name *only;* then your *will* would make sure it passes to your children. But remember, if you keep the house in just your own name and you do *not* have a will, it will go via intestate succession (see page 8) and your second husband will most likely end up with a portion of it as well. If you want to protect your kids, make sure that you have everything you own in just your name and you designate via a legal document who is to inherit it.

Q. What is probate?

A. In all states, if all you have is a will, when you die it has to go through a court procedure known as *probate*. For instance, let's say that my mom owns a home and she wants me to have it when she dies. She leaves it to me via a will that she has had a lawyer draw up. After my mom dies, even though the will says I am to get the house, the deed to the house is still in her name, and she is no longer alive and able to sign that deed over to me. Yes, the will says I am to get it, that is not the problem; the problem is how does the deed of the house get put into my name when it is still in her name? That is where the probate court comes in. The procedure in most states will work like this: Someone (usually the lawyer or executor) has to take the will down to the court and first have the judge authenticate the will—in other words, make sure that this will is valid. After that is done, the judge will sign over on my mother's behalf all her property to the rightful beneficiaries (such as me). For that simple procedure, there will be in most states substantial fees involved: court costs of about $1,000 as well as a variety of expenses here and there. When all is said and done, this process not only can take from six months to two years or more, but it is also extremely costly. For instance, if my mom lived in the state of California, and her home was worth $200,000, regardless of how large a mortgage she carried, the probate fees would be $10,300. That's right—even if this house of hers had a $190,000 mortgage, the probate fees are based on the fair market value (what it would sell for) of this house, which in this case was $200,000. That is a lot of money to spend, especially when there is a legal way to avoid spending it, which I'll talk about in a minute.

Q. Is a will the only way to make sure that my children or loved ones get my possessions and money?

A. No. Besides a will, one other way is to have a revocable living trust. A revocable living trust is a different kind of legal document that can ensure that your possessions and money will go to the people you want them to go to. In fact, in many cases it is far better to have a trust than it is to have just a will.

TRUSTS

Q. What is a revocable living trust, and how is it different from a will?

A. A will is a document that directs where your assets will go after your death. A revocable living trust is something that holds your assets while you are alive. You put your assets into the trust, almost as if you were putting them into a safe. You can do whatever you want with them while you're alive. Then, after you die, the safe can be opened and your beneficiaries can receive your possessions, according to your instructions.

You create a trust with a legal document similar to a will. And as with a will, you can change your trust at any time. But a big difference between a will and a trust is that, with a trust, *your estate does not go through probate*. Because you have already transferred the ownership of your assets to the trust, there is no need for a judge to be involved in changing the title of these assets. If, in the example on page 12, my mother had simply created a revocable living trust while she was alive and signed the deed to her home over to this trust to be held for me after her death, I would not have to wait six months to two years to get the house. I would get it immediately. Also it would cost me nothing in probate fees to get it, saving me $10,300.

Q. Is a revocable living trust complicated to set up?

A. No. You create one just as you would a will. You can have a lawyer do it for you, or use one of the myriad books or computer programs to help guide you through the procedure. It is always wise, however, to make sure that if you do it yourself you have your documents reviewed by a lawyer to make sure that you did it correctly. If you have a sizable estate, I would recommend having a lawyer do it from the start. The importance of setting up the trust and funding it properly (which I'll talk about next) means it is probably worth the expense of having an attorney do the paperwork.

Q. How much does it cost to have a revocable living trust created by a lawyer?

A. Most revocable living trusts cost around $500 to $1,500 to set up and fund. The more assets you have, the more it will usually cost. Do not let a lawyer charge you by the hour to create a trust for you. It should be one set price that you agree upon ahead of time.

Q. What does it mean to "fund" a revocable living trust? To have an empty trust?

A. Remember when I said my mom should have signed over the title of her house to the name of the trust? That would be *funding* the trust. When your trust is first drawn up, all you have is a bunch of papers with a lot of words on them saying who is to get what when. What makes it different from a will is that *you actually transfer your assets into the name of the trust while you are still alive.* A judge does not have to transfer the titles for you after you have died. This transfer of your money and possessions into the trust is called funding the trust. It is very important that everything that you own is held in the name of the trust. If you simply draw up the trust and do not fund it, then in essence your trust is empty. If this is the case when you die, then everything still has to be dictated by your will if you have one. Not funding a trust is one of the biggest mistakes that people make when it comes to trusts, and it happens all the time. *If you don't fund your trust, you will be wasting the effort and money that you put into creating it.*

Q. How do I make sure I fund my trust correctly?

A. If I were you, I would have a lawyer draw up the trust, and make sure that he or she be the one to fund it. In fact, handling the paperwork of funding is the most complicated part of creating the trust. The fee that you pay to your attorney should include his funding the trust for you.

Q. If I go to a lawyer to do this, what should I expect to have done for me?

A. Most trusts are boiler plates, meaning that when you go to see the lawyer, he or she has a document that is already in their computer that they simply use over and over again. When lawyers create a trust for you, they simply personalize it for you. They change the names and property to fit your wishes and desires, but there is usually no need to create a new trust from scratch each time. This process should take an hour or two at most.

What you are really paying them for, then, is first to sit down with you after the trust has been drawn up and explain everything to you about how it works; and second, to fund the trust or transfer all your assets into the name of the trust for you. Third, at the same time that you create the trust, you should have a *backup will,* also called a *pour-over will,* drawn up. (I'll explain this later.) Make sure that all three of the above are included in the price that your attorney quotes to you before you start.

Q. What does the term *revocable living trust* mean?

A. It's a *trust* because you are trusting this entity with the title to your possessions. It's called *revocable* because you can change it at any time while you are alive. And it's *living* because you create it while you are alive, and because it lives on after you, making sure your goods go where you intended.

Q. What do you mean that the revocable living trust can go on living after I have died?

A. Since you have put everything in trust, while you are alive you can write instructions into the trust as to how and when you want your assets to be distributed. Let's say you have children who are not currently very responsible with money, and you are afraid that if you were to die and they were to get everything that you had, they would take it and blow it all within about two months. Your wish is that it could be kept safe for them until they were, say, forty years of age. With a revocable living trust, you could easily do this. You simply appoint a *successor trustee,* someone to make the decisions over the money in the trust and carry out your wishes for you after you are gone. Many parents find this an incredible side benefit of the revocable living trust.

Q. Is having a revocable living trust going to make my tax returns complicated?

A. No, this kind of trust is considered to be the same as you. So just as you file tax returns now, whether single or married, the same will be true for the trust. Once you set up the revocable living trust, you will not notice even one iota of difference in how things are with or without one. The difference is not felt when you are living; it is felt after you have died.

Q. So is the only reason to set up a living trust to help my beneficiaries?

A. No. There is another reason for you to have your assets in trust while you are alive. Even though we do not like to think about it, death is not the only mishap that can happen in life. There is always a possibility that we could be incapacitated at any time. Suppose you own your home with your spouse in JTWROS (see page 11) and you feel great because you know that if your spouse were to die or vice versa, this house would pass to each of you without probate or costs, and right away. "This is all I own, so I don't need a trust," you may think. You are correct *if all that ever happens is that one of you dies.*

But now suppose that your spouse is hit by a car or has a stroke and is permanently incapacitated. You may need to sell the house because you can no longer afford it with just your income, and so you put it on the market. However, *you cannot now sell your house.* Your incapacitated spouse cannot sign his or her name to the deed that his or her name is on. To sell the house, assuming you do not have a durable power of attorney, you are going to have to go down to the court, have your spouse declared incompetent—this will cost around $5,000—and once you do sell the house, every time you want to do something with your spouse's half of that money, you are going to have to get permission from the courts. This is a terrible situation to find yourself in.

And you could avoid it if you had a revocable living trust with an incapacity clause, which states that in the event you or your spouse were to become incompetent or incapacitated, you would be able to sign for your spouse (or vice versa) without having to go to court or paying a conservatorship fee. You don't need to be married to have such a clause, by the way. If you are unmarried and have a revocable living trust with an incapacity clause in it, then you could name anyone you want to be able to step in and take care of your financial affairs. The same is true even if you are married. So, as you can see, a revocable living trust can be as much a benefit to you as it will be to those you leave behind.

Q. Does everything I own get put into my revocable living trust?

A. Everything that has a title to it, such as your bank accounts, brokerage accounts, and all your real estate. However, things such as your furniture or knickknacks—things that do not have a title to them—will simply be covered by your backup will.

Q. If I have a revocable living trust, do I need a will?

A. Yes. When you have a trust, a will serves as a backup for all those things that you either forgot or did not get around to or did not have a title so you could not put them into the trust. It is for this reason that when you have a trust, your will is known as a backup will or a pour-over will. Whatever is not covered by the trust is poured over into the will.

Q. How do I know I need a trust or if a will is just fine?

A. In general, if you have real estate valued at more than $60,000 to $100,000 (the cutoff number varies from state to state, so check the law where you live), and if all you have is a will, your assets will have to go through the long version of probate. If you're under the cutoff, then you still have to go through probate, but it can be done simply by filling out what's called a *probate affidavit*. This is relatively simple paperwork that takes just a matter of days and hardly costs anything at all. But before you count on a probate affidavit to save you lots of time and money, take a careful look at the value of your assets, especially if you have real estate. It might easily have crept up past the $100,000 mark in value, and if that's the case, you should definitely check out the benefits of a revocable living trust. If you don't have real estate valued at more than $60,000 to $100,000, then for your other assets, look under pay-on-death accounts, pages 23–24.

Q. Will a revocable living trust save me money on my estate tax?

A. No. A revocable living trust saves you only probate fees and time. Estate taxes can be saved with what is known as an *AB* or *credit shelter trust*. If you have an estate worth more than $600,000, make sure you see an attorney to ask about this kind of a trust, for it can save you up to $235,000 in estate taxes.

Q. Why does my attorney tell me that I do not need a revocable living trust?

A. In many states attorney fees are set by statute. Meaning that it has already been determined how much you will have to pay your attorney to probate your will for you—in most cases, this is a large sum of money. Usually, then, it is not to your attorney's financial benefit for you to have a revocable living trust. To find out if this lawyer is being honest with you, ask him or her to write down on his or her letterhead answers to the following questions (make sure you keep the letter in your files):

   ⇾ How much will it cost me to have a will drawn up (if you do not have one already)?

   ⇾ If I (and my spouse) were to die today and all I (we) had was a will, how much would it cost my beneficiaries in total to probate my estate in its entirety?

⇥ How much would it cost me to create and fund a revocable living trust?

⇥ If I had a revocable living trust, and the same thing were to happen, that I (and my spouse) were to die, how much in total would it cost my beneficiaries to get my estate?

Add up the total it will cost your beneficiaries if you had a revocable living trust, then add this figure to the fee to create one and compare this number to the costs to your beneficiaries if you had only a will. The answer will be easy. Whichever costs less in the long run is the way to go.

DESIGNATING YOUR BENEFICIARIES

This section deals with some things you should know about how to leave to those that you want to have it, your hard-earned money, in the most secure and efficient ways.

Q. What if all I have in my estate are bank accounts and retirement accounts totaling over $100,000 but I do not own any real estate? Do I still need a revocable living trust?

A. In this case, actually, you do not. Whenever you have a bank account you can ask the bank to make it a pay-on-death (POD) account. To do this, you specify in writing to the bank or institution where your money is held to whom they should pay out these funds upon your death. Because you'll have already signed papers doing this, when you die these funds will pass immediately to your beneficiaries and will totally avoid the time and costs of probate. The same is true with any retirement account or life-insurance policy, for that matter. Whenever you have an account in which they ask you to name a beneficiary, this account will not go through probate. So if this is the situation, you do not need a revocable living trust.

Q. What if I cannot decide right now on whom I want to leave my money to? Can I have the POD, retirement account, or life-insurance policy paid to my estate?

A. NO, NO, NO! This is a big mistake. If you name your estate as the beneficiary and if all you have is a will, then you have thrown that asset back into probate court. Whatever you do, when you use a POD or have the chance to name a designated beneficiary, in most cases make sure that you use the name of an actual person to whom you want to leave something. Remember you can always change your mind and designate a new beneficiary.

Q. What if I have a revocable living trust? Is it okay to make the trust the primary beneficiary of my retirement account? I am married and want my spouse to be protected.

A. Again, no! With any retirement account that you have—whether it's a 401(k), a 403(b), a TSA, an IRA, or a Keogh plan, make sure the primary beneficiary is your spouse. After that, it is okay to name your living trust as the contingent beneficiary (the one who gets everything if the primary beneficiary is not living). This is because when you are married, your spouse has certain rights that a trust does not have. Remember that the money in your retirement accounts is money that you have never paid taxes on up till that point. And the government, being eager to get its tax money, has some interesting rules that apply to these funds after you die.

If your spouse is the primary beneficiary, he or she can continue to defer taxes on these funds by simply taking over the account as if it were his or hers, or rolling it over into an account with his or her name on it, or a variety of other maneuvers. In most cases, your spouse can continue to defer taxes on these funds for many years to come. For anyone besides your spouse, however, this is not true. *Any other beneficiary—including your trust, if that's what you name—will have a maximum of five years from the date of death to make sure that all the funds in the retirement account are withdrawn.* If you have a large sum of money within your retirement accounts, this will mean your beneficiaries will have quite a hefty tax bill, which is the exact intent of the IRS. So if you make the primary beneficiary of your retirement accounts your revocable living trust—even if the trust says everything goes to your spouse and even if your spouse controls the trust after you die—those accounts will have to be wiped clean in five years and have taxes paid on them. So whatever you do—if you are married—when it comes to a retirement account, make sure that the primary beneficiary is your spouse and the trust is a secondary one.

Q. Should I make my spouse my primary beneficiary rather than my revocable living trust on accounts that are not retirement accounts? My life-insurance policy, for example, or my POD accounts at the bank?

A. In this case it is just fine to make your beneficiary the revocable living trust if you have one. Upon your death with these accounts, there are usually no tax consequences to your beneficiaries. If you do not have a revocable living trust, you can name your spouse or any other individual.

GIFTING

It's easy to feel overwhelmed by the whole business of wills and trusts, and many people are tempted to start giving away money to their children to seemingly avoid the whole problem. Others think that they will outsmart the system by simply adding their child's name to the property that they want to pass on. This is often a serious mistake. As you will see, gifting or putting your child's name on an asset can create a real mess for both of you. Sometimes the mess can be cleaned up, but other times this move can backfire in a disastrous way.

A gift is meant to be a thing of joy. Please read this section and learn from the questions that others have asked, to make sure that for you and your loved ones it stays just that.

Q. How much can I gift a year without having to file a gift tax return?

A. You can give $10,000 a year to as many individuals as you like without incurring any gift tax. If you have three children, four brothers, five cousins, twenty-five friends— you can give $10,000 to each one of those people. If you are married, your spouse can give $10,000 per year to as many people as he or she wants to as well.

Q. What happens if I give more than $10,000 in one year to someone?

A. Anytime you give someone more than $10,000, then you have to file what is known as a gift-tax return. In addition to the $10,000-per-year, per-person gift exemption, you can currently give away up to a grand total of $600,000 over your lifetime. If you have not given this amount away by the time you die, you can leave the balance of that $600,000 divided among as many people as you wish. Note that is not $600,000 to each person, that is a *total* of $600,000. If at your death you leave more than $600,000 (and do not have a tax-planning trust in place), then your beneficiaries will owe estate taxes.

If you give someone more than $10,000 a year, whatever amount you give them above that $10,000 will be subtracted from the $600,000. For example, suppose your house is worth $320,000, and you and your spouse give it to your daughter by simply taking your names off the title and putting her name on. In essence you have just given your child a gift of $320,000. Since you are allowed to each give her $10,000 a year, or $20,000 between the two of you, you have given her $300,000 more than the allowable amount. Therefore you will have to file a gift-tax return for $300,000. This $300,000 can be subtracted from your allowable $600,000, which will leave you with $300,000 that you can still give away tax-free while you are alive, or after you have died.

Q. Is it a good idea to give my children my house or other assets while I am still alive?

A. It will depend on why you are doing it. If you are doing it for estate-tax-planning reasons, then it could be a fantastic idea. However, this is something that you should never do without consulting a lawyer who specializes in estate planning. If you're in a position to do this, you probably have an estate worth well over $600,000. If your estate is worth less than $600,000, it usually makes very little sense to give your assets to your children before your death, because you can pass them on free of estate tax anyway.

Q. What if I want to avoid the hassle of a will and a revocable living trust altogether and I just put my kids' names on my house and accounts as joint tenants. Will that do the trick?

A. If you do this, you could be asking for a whole lot *more* hassle without your even being aware of it. Let's say that you simply put your children's names on your home, and you think, "Great, when I die it will pass directly to my kids without all that red tape!" That will be true as long as nothing happens before your death. But in doing this, you have opened up yourself to another potential problem.

Suppose your son is in a serious car accident in which he injures another person. The injured person retains representation of a very sharp lawyer who very easily finds out (since all titles to real estate are of public record) that your son owns a house. Yes, this real estate may be your home, but since you put his name on it, your son legally owns it as well. Your child is sued, and before you even know what has happened, you might find that *your* house, *your* home, is no longer yours. Or suppose your daughter's name is on your bank account and she (or even her husband!) gets in terrible tax trouble. You might find the IRS emptying *your* money from that bank account. This can apply to real estate, bank accounts, and anything else that also has your child's name on it.

Q. My widowed mom gave me her home and all her stocks before she went into a nursing home a few months ago, and she has since died. Do I owe estate tax and income tax on what she left me?

A. You will owe estate tax if the house and all her stocks and cash total more than $600,000 in value. On every dollar above that $600,000, up to $3,000,000, you will owe between 37 percent and 55 percent. After $3,000,000, it is all taxed at 55 percent. The IRS may be generous with the first $600,000, but after that you are going to pay dearly.

Income tax is another issue, however. If you inherit assets such as stocks or real estate, they will not be taxed until you sell them. How much you're taxed then will depend on whether you inherited that asset after the death of the owner, or if the owner gave it to you while he or she was still alive, as your mom did. Here is the difference—and it is a big difference.

INHERITED ASSETS

When you inherit something from a person who has died, you get what is called a step up in cost basis on the asset that you inherited. This may sound like Greek to you, but let me try to explain it in plain English. If, for example, your mom bought her home many years ago for $20,000, that figure is her *cost basis* for that asset. Let's say she kept the house in her name, and when she died she left it to you via her revocable living trust or will. Because you inherited the house after she died, for tax purposes *your* cost basis becomes what the value of the house was worth when she died. If the house was worth $300,000 at the time you took over the title, your cost basis in the house would be $300,000. In other words, you got a step up in basis from her original $20,000, to $300,000. So if you were to sell the house you would owe only income taxes on any amount above that $300,000—not bad.

RECEIVING ASSETS AS GIFTS

If, however, your mom gave you her home and other assets while she was still alive, *along with the title to that house and other assets comes her original cost basis as well.* If Mom's original cost basis in her house was $20,000, that is now your cost basis as well. If you sell the house today for $300,000, you will owe income taxes on $280,000—

about $78,000. OUCH. So, as you can see, there is a huge income tax difference between gifting and inheriting an asset that has appreciated in value over the years. This is why, with assets that were purchased for far less than they are worth today, if you plan to sell them, inheriting them after death is the best way to receive them.

In most cases, then, it is far better to simply give cash while you are alive than to give an asset that has gone up in value since you originally purchased it.

Q. My parents gifted to me in total an apartment building, so from what you have said, I will have to pay a large capital gains tax if I choose to sell it. They're still alive, so can I put the building back in their name so I can inherit it instead?

A. This is a very difficult question. You see, when they gifted you the apartment building, they should have filed a gift-tax return (and most likely did). Undoubtedly the apartment building is worth more than the $10,000 that each of them is allowed to give you tax-free. To use the same numbers as in the previous question, let's say the apartment building was worth $320,000. Their gift-tax return will have been for $300,000 (that's the value of the building, $320,000, minus their combined exemption of $20,000). What this also means is that if they have no other tax-planning trusts set up, they have used up $300,000 of the $600,000 that they will be allowed to leave you estate-tax-free.

What happens if you now give this apartment building back to them? First, since *you* can only give *them* each $10,000 a year, you will also have to file a gift-tax return for $300,000—using up half of *your* $600,000 allotment as well. Now, when your parents die, estate taxes will be owed on anything that they leave over $300,000. Since the apartment building you want to give back to them is worth this much, if they have anything else to leave you besides this, you will pay 37 percent to 55 percent of that amount to the IRS. Not to mention that if you want to leave the building and anything else to your own children, you're going to have the same problem.

As you can see, by gifting without thinking about the ramifications, you have gotten yourself into a big pickle. I would suggest leaving everything just as it is. The worst case is that you are going to have to pay capital-gains tax of 28 percent when you sell the building. But 28 percent is better than 37 percent and a lot better than 55 percent. From now on, don't you or your parents do anything like this without consulting an estate-planning lawyer!

Q. My mother has already put my name on her residence as a joint tenant. What must I do now to take my name off the title, or is it too late?

A. If your mom has simply added your name to her title as a joint tenant, for example, because no money passed hands and you never took possession of the house, you can simply quitclaim the house back to her and everything will be back to normal.

POWER OF ATTORNEY

Maybe the one thing we hate thinking about even more than death is illness or incapacity. We all, and this includes me, prefer to imagine that we'll just go on living our lives in good health in both body and mind until one day we peacefully drop dead. That's what I wish for myself, anyway—but I know it's quite possible that my wish will not come true.

Being unable to take care of yourself, whether because of aging or a sudden accident, is never easy to deal with. But if this should happen to you or to someone you love, the situation is even worse if they can't take care of themselves financially, either. Who will sign the checks? Pay the bills? Manage the money? My callers are always worried about these kinds of questions. How can we guarantee you will never be incapacitated financially even if you are personally? Follow the suggestions made in this section to protect yourself and your family from tragedy.

Q. Should I put my name on my parents' accounts to make sure that I could sign for them in case of an incapacity?

A. It will depend somewhat on the size of the estate, but in most cases you are far better off preparing for an incapacity by using an incapacity clause within a living revocable trust (page 13), or by having a durable power of attorney drawn up.

Q. What is the difference between a power of attorney and a durable power of attorney?

A. A power of attorney indicates that you have authorized someone to act on your behalf. This designated person is known as the *attorney in fact*. The authority granted by a power of attorney can be very wide or strictly limited. For instance, it can give a person only the right to sell your home for you while you are out of town. Or it could be very broad in its scope, and allow that person to do anything that you could do—sign checks, pay bills, withdraw money from any and all of your accounts. Keep in mind that *most regular powers of attorney become null and void the moment the person who created the document becomes incompetent.* The durable power of attorney does everything that the power of attorney does. However, *the durable power of attorney remains valid even if the one who created it becomes incompetent.* Since this is the main reason that most people have this kind of a document, in case of an incompetency, the difference between these two can be HUGE.

Q. My father had a durable power of attorney drawn up and made my sister attorney in fact. My father is now in a nursing home and my sister is spending all of his money on herself. Is there anything we can do about it?

A. You've just seen one of the drawbacks of a power of attorney of any kind. In theory, it is very easy legally to revoke a durable power of attorney. In practice, it can be very difficult, and a lot of damage can be done in the meantime.

If the durable power of attorney was recorded, meaning it was taken down to the county recorder's office and entered there just like the deed to your house, then you must also record the revocation as well. In some states, all the person who created the durable power of attorney has to do is to declare either in writing or orally (preferably with a witness present) that he or she no longer wants the attorney in fact to continue acting in that role. However, it's not always this simple. Even if your father were to tell your sister he no longer wanted her to act on his behalf, would the bank know that he did that? Not necessarily. So she could go down there with her piece of paper and continue to draw money out. Even if he were to ask her to return the document that gave her this power to begin with, she could have made many, many copies of it. (Yes, many institutions will accept a copy of the original.)

When you create a durable power of attorney, you may be letting a genie out of a bottle—it's not so easy to put the genie back in. You may be granting someone the broadest range of power over all your affairs. Before you do this, it is essential that you think long and hard about how much you trust the person you are going to ask to act on your behalf. You have to know without a shadow of a doubt that that person has not only your best interest at heart, but that of the other family members as well, and that that person has the maturity and judgment equal to this responsibility. In your case, you may be able to get your father to revoke this power of attorney in writing, but most likely you will need to get the help of a real attorney to help you sort this one out.

Q. Can more than one person be given a durable power of attorney where they can each act separately?

A. Yes. You could give a durable power of attorney to as many people as you like. But I would be very hesitant to do this. As I said in the answer above, each one of these people has the right to sign for you and act fully on your behalf. Also, can you imagine the confusion that would be caused if two people, each with your power of attorney in hand, came into the same bank and said they represented you? In this case it would not surprise me if the bank decided not to honor either of them.

If your parents are very old, they might want to give each other a durable power of attorney, and perhaps give one to you as well. I can't think of many other cases where it would make sense to designate more than one attorney in fact.

Q. I have a durable power of attorney and when I took it in to the bank, they refused to honor it. Does this happen often?

A. Yes. It happens often enough that in the state of California, for instance, there has been a statute passed that says if an institution does not accept the durable power of attorney in the same efficient way they accept other legal documents, and if you have to get a lawyer to make them accept it, the institution—here, your bank—will be liable for your legal fees. I suspect it's because powers of attorney are so easily abused that banks are wary of honoring them. But if you have a durable power of attorney for a legitimate reason, it can be a real problem if someone does not honor it. That is one reason why I like using an incapacity clause within a living revocable trust rather than a durable power of attorney.

Q. Is there a way that I can make sure that my uncle, who has my mother's durable power of attorney, is spending the money in an appropriate way?

A. This is a lot harder than it seems. In most states, to get an accounting with a durable power of attorney, you would have to file a civil lawsuit to get the information you want. This is another reason that I like doing this whole process through a living revocable trust. If your uncle was the trustee over your mother's living revocable trust and you wanted to make sure that he was using the money properly, all you would have to do is petition the probate court and they would do an accounting according to the rules that your mom set up in her trust while she was competent. This is a lot easier than having to sue in court.

Q. Can I have a durable power of attorney where the attorney in fact is two people who must act jointly before they can do anything?

A. Yes, you can. But think about this carefully, because even though this might give you mental comfort knowing that you have a check-and-balance system seemingly in place, there's a drawback if someone has to act immediately on your behalf. Sometimes having to get two signatures can cause delays that might be significant.

Q. What if I do not want anyone to be able to sign for me unless I really cannot do it for myself?

A. It is true that unless you state so in the document, as soon as you draw up a durable power of attorney, you are giving someone the right to cash checks, buy and sell stocks, withdraw cash, or sell your home right out from under you. Since this exposure makes most people feel a little vulnerable (and who could blame them?), you should make absolutely sure, as I said before, that you give this document only to someone you trust with your life. What you can do is to have a third party (whom you also trust) hold this document for you until the time comes (if ever) that you would want that person to use it, and then at that time have it given to them and recorded.

Q. My parents' lawyer suggests I have a "springing" power of attorney for them. What is this?

A. This is a power of attorney that becomes effective, or "springs" into action, only when you become incapacitated. I don't like springing powers of attorney for two reasons: First, a springing power of attorney is not yet valid in all states. Second, in the states where it is accepted, there's the potential problem of deciding when someone is really incompetent. So in my opinion, rather than springing into action, it springs into creating a myriad of possible problems. You are far better off having a durable power of attorney with someone you trust.

Q. How much does it cost to obtain a durable power of attorney?

A. Anywhere from $25 to $100, with the average cost being around $50.

Q. If I live in New York and my parents live in Idaho, will a durable power of attorney from New York work for them?

A. Every state has its own individual form and rules governing the use of a durable power of attorney. Not only are the rules different but how they must be signed and how they are legally recorded are different as well. It is better to have an attorney in the state that Mom and Pop live in draw up this document for you.

Q. I had a durable power of attorney drawn up about fifteen years ago. Is it still valid?

A. The laws in regard to a durable power of attorney are constantly changing. Therefore—and this goes for any legal document—you should have it reviewed by an attorney every few years. Your power of attorney should still be, but may not be, as comprehensive as it could be. Go have it checked out just to be sure. This is far too important a document to play guessing games with.

MEDICAID/MEDICARE

About 40 percent of all the people who are in nursing homes today are covered by Medicaid. Medicaid is a state- and federally funded program designed to help cover medical and nursing home costs for less affluent Americans. Even though in theory Medicaid sounds great, the truth is that you have to be close to financial devastation in order to qualify. Medicare is our federal health insurance program for people sixty-five and over who collect Social Security and covers more than 30 million people. This too is a wonderful idea, but again, it can be dangerous to put too much reliance on this kind of assistance, especially if what you need is nursing home care. This section deals with questions that often come up about both Medicaid and Medicare.

Q. My mother took her name off everything—her home, brokerage account, bank account, etc.—and put everything into my name so that she could qualify for Medicaid in case of a nursing home stay. How does this impact my own financial life?

A. Well, it will depend on many things. But the main question is how it will affect the quality of your *mother's* life in the long run. Many people try to get rid of their assets this way, hoping that if they have to spend some time in a nursing home, the state will pay for them. I do not encourage this. First of all, the care you'll receive in many nursing homes under Medicaid may be not as good as the care you will get if you are a private-pay patient. It drives me crazy to think that someone who's in a nursing home at the close of her days—when she ought to have as much comfort and quality of life as she can—is going to have less, all for the sake of MONEY.

Furthermore, it is never a good idea to give away everything. Now your mother is completely dependent upon you, and what if something happens to you? Did she think about that? I am not against gifting in certain circumstances, but I would never advocate getting rid of it all, particularly in this kind of effort to beat the system.

In regard to your question of how this impacts you financially, it will all depend on the cost basis of the assets she transferred to you (see question on page 31). You may find that you will owe considerable tax on these funds and real estate when you go to sell them. Also, if these investments generate taxable income, you will have to pay income taxes on these funds at your tax bracket; in fact, the income from these investments may kick you up to a higher bracket altogether. The other problem (see page 29) is that if you were to be sued, a lawyer might attach all of your assets, including those that your mom is hiding under your name, and if they were successful in getting a judgment, your mom could lose everything.

Q. My husband is about to go into a nursing home. What are the areas that I need to look into to know if I qualify for Medicaid to help cover the costs?

A. Wow, that is a question I could write a whole book about—in fact, there are several available on this subject. To give you a *very* short summary, the following is what must be in place for a person to qualify for Medicaid in relation to paying for a nursing home stay:

The person must:

➤ be a resident in the state that would provide Medicaid benefits

➤ be at least sixty-five years of age, or disabled or blind

➤ have only a certain amount of income and assets and need the type of care that is provided in a nursing home

These are the requirements at the time this book is being written, but be aware that the rules concerning Medicaid frequently change and may vary depending on your state. I would suggest you look at Armand D. Budish's *Avoiding the Medicaid Trap* and consult with an attorney specializing in elder care.

Q. Does being married affect the amount of income or assets required to qualify for Medicaid? I am married now, but if my wife or I died, would that change the Medicaid status of the surviving spouse?

A. This is a good question. In dealing with Medicaid, you are far better off knowing way beforehand what needs to be done rather than waiting until the last moment.

Yes, the rules for qualification are different when you are married versus when you are not. I can give a brief summary, but I recommend you ask the guidance of a professional in your state, for every state has its own quirks. Here are some general rules.

IF YOU'RE UNMARRIED

When it comes to Medicaid, all your income, whether earned or unearned, is taken into consideration. This includes your Social Security, alimony, pension, worker's compensation, annuities, unemployment, interest, gifts, dividends, etc.

What state you live in is a key question. There are about thirty-three states where there is no limit on the amount of income you can have before qualifying for

Medicaid. In general, in these states Medicaid will pay for nursing home care if your income is less than the cost of the nursing home. However, in the other eighteen states, your income must be below a limit set by state law. If you live in one of the following states, make sure that you see someone who specializes in elder care law to help you figure everything out:

ALABAMA
ALASKA
ARIZONA
ARKANSAS
COLORADO
DELAWARE
FLORIDA
IDAHO
IOWA
LOUISIANA
MISSISSIPPI
NEVADA
NEW JERSEY
NEW MEXICO
OKLAHOMA
SOUTH DAKOTA
TEXAS

If you are eligible for Medicaid, almost all of your income except for a small amount (thirty to seventy-five dollars, depending on the state) for personal needs will go to pay for your nursing home bill. If that is not enough to cover the expenses, then Medicaid will step in and take over the deficit. If your nursing home stay is going to be a short one, six months or less, then Medicaid may also allow you to keep a few hundred dollars per month to help maintain your home that you are expected to return to.

Besides the income test, you will also have to pass what is called the *asset limitation test*. In most cases for unmarried individuals, almost all your assets must be turned over to the nursing home before Medicaid will pay for you.

What you are allowed to keep in most states and still qualify is your personal home, as long as you intend to return there or a relative or spouse is living there. You can also keep a few other things, such as your car, regardless of what it is worth, if you use it to get to work or to get medical care. Otherwise, you can still keep it as long as it is not worth more than $4,500. Again, there are many other rules about what you can or cannot keep, but the bottom line is that if you are unmarried, you will have to spend almost everything in order to qualify.

If you are married, the story is a little better, but not much.

IF YOU ARE MARRIED

Just like an unmarried individual, you also have to pass the income eligibility test. The hard question for married people is, How is income split up in order to calculate eligibility for Medicaid? In most states, the answer is known as the "name of the check rule," which works just the way it sounds: Whatever checks are made out in your own name are considered to belong to you. So if your wife gets a Social Security check and a pension check with just her name on it, as far as Medicaid is concerned, it's considered her income *even if you put it in a joint account and spend it on both of you.* If you get a pension check with your name on it, the same holds true. Income from interest and dividends in an account with both of your names on it is considered to be split equally between the two of you.

Now please note that this is different from state to state, especially for those people who happen to live in community-property states—Arizona, California, Idaho, Louisiana, Nevada, New Mexico, Texas, and Washington. In these states it is entirely possible that all your income, regardless of whose name appears on the check, will be considered as equally divided between the two of you.

Once all income is considered, the spouse who remains at home will be given what is known as a basic living allowance. This is the amount of money that he or she is allowed to keep and that does not have to go toward the nursing home. The intent behind this allowance is to make sure that the spouse at home is not totally impoverished. This amount is different in each state and is determined by a complicated formula. I won't try to give the formulas here, they are so intricate and frustrating. I would urge you to check with an elder care lawyer in your area to find out this figure for you.

In most cases the easy part is passing the income test—as long as you have income that is less than the cost of a nursing home or the income cap for your particular state, you will probably qualify. The hard part is passing the asset eligibility test. In brief, this is what you need to know: Your assets such as your home, car, personal effects, etc., are protected. Married couples can keep a significant amount in investments and/or cash as well. They have a major advantage over unmarried people: An unmarried person can have only about $2,000 while a married couple can keep around $80,000.

But whether you are married or not, no matter what state you live in, there are still many drawbacks to paying for nursing home care with Medicaid, for most of your money has to be gone before Medicaid will start to pay.

Q. I live in North Dakota, and I want to move my sister from Illinois to a nursing home close to me so I can go and visit her every day. How do I establish residency for her so that she can meet that particular qualification for Medicaid?

A. Fortunately, this is easy. When you want to become a resident of a state, all you have to do is move there with the intent of staying indefinitely. So if your sister comes to North Dakota and plans to stay in the nursing home for the foreseeable future, she becomes a resident of your state. As long as she meets all the other criteria, she will immediately be able to attain Medicaid benefits.

Q. What if my wife and I don't want to have to give up our hard-earned money? Can't we just give it to our kids and then apply for Medicaid?

A. Wrong as can be. Did your grandmother ever tell you "you can't eat your cake and have it, too"? The government is not going to hand over thousands of dollars for your medical expenses casually. They're going to check on you. First, there is what is called a *look-back rule*. This means that the government will look back into time to see what you have given away to your children, or anyone else for that matter, in the past thirty-six months (more about this in the next question). If you have given away anything in order to qualify, you will be deemed ineligible for a period of time. And as of January 1, 1997, if you give away money just in order to qualify for Medicaid, and you are caught doing so, it will now be considered a criminal offense.

Q. My father signed over $175,000 worth of stock to me fourteen months ago. He now needs to go into a

nursing home. When will it be safe for him to apply for Medicaid?

A. Whatever you do, do not apply before the thirty-six months are up from the date he gave you the stock, or sixty months if your father happened to have had that stock in a living revocable trust. Make sure that you are very clear as to when this time period is up. If you happen to apply for Medicaid before then, your father could be disqualified for a considerable time from receiving Medicaid as well as be guilty of a criminal offense.

Q. My parents transferred $200,000 from their name to mine and then immediately applied for Medicaid. Of course they were caught. Now how long will they be barred from qualifying for Medicaid? Just thirty-six months, right?

A. Wrong. The answer depends on how much money they transferred or the value of the assets. Let's take that $200,000 worth of stock and cash they gave you. The state will take an average-per-month cost of what nursing homes run in their area and divide that monthly figure into the value of the gift you received. If the average price of a nursing home in your area is $4,000, they'd divide that into $200,000 and get 50. This means that for fifty months from the date the gift was first made, your parents will not be considered eligible for Medicaid.

Q. When does the period of ineligibility for Medicaid start?

A. It will depend on your state. Some states date the ineligibility period from the date you made the transfer or gift, other states date it from the month after you made the gift. So if you made a gift on January 1, 1993, and applied to Medicaid too soon, and they said that you will be ineligible for, let's say, fifty months, that means fifty months from January 1, 1993, in some states or February 1, 1993, in other states.

Q. I heard that even if I qualify for Medicaid, the state can put a lien against my property in order to get their money back after I die. Is this true?

A. I am afraid that it may well be true. Right now not many states are doing it, even though they have the right to do so under the OBRA 1993 Act, but this does not mean that they will not in the future. However, they can go after assets only in the name of the person receiving Medicaid, not assets owned by the spouse. Nor can the state go after the house—even if it's in the name of the person receiving Medicaid—if the spouse is living in it, or unless they can prove that you will never be returning to your home. There are other restrictions as well, but this is another one of those areas where I urge you to make sure you seek the professional help of an elder care attorney.

MEDICARE

Q. My aunt tells me that if she needs to go into a nursing home Medicare will pay for her stay now that she is over sixty-five. Is this true?

A. NO, NO, NO! This is a common and dangerous misunderstanding. Medicare *rarely* pays for nursing home insurance. Less than *2 percent* of all those people in nursing homes are covered by Medicare. Yet your aunt is not alone; almost 80 percent of all people asked think that Medicare will cover them if they have a long-term-care stay. Please know that this is not true. This is what has to happen for Medicare to pay for her long-term-care stay. First of all, she has got to be in a hospital for three days prior to entering a nursing home. Next, she has to be admitted into a *skilled nursing care* facility. This means it must have services that can be performed by or under the supervision of nurses, physical therapists, or other medically trained professionals. Most people in a nursing home today are in what is known as a *custodial care* facility, meaning a place where the staff helps people dress, bathe, eat, take medications, and carry on other normal living activities, but these skills do not require medical training. The chances your aunt will be admitted to a skilled nursing facility are very, very small unless her medical circumstances are exceptional.

Finally, even if she does meet those two criteria,

Medicare will pay in full for only the first twenty days of her stay. After that, for the next eighty days, she will have to pay roughly the first ninety dollars a day and Medicare would cover the rest. But after a hundred days, Medicare will stop cold. Your aunt will be totally responsible for the nursing home costs—which are likely to be much higher in a skilled care facility than in a regular nursing home.

Q. If Medicare won't pay for my nursing home stay, will it pay for my care at home?

A. Maybe. In order for Medicare to pay for care at home, your needs must be certified by a doctor, and as part of this care you must need part-time or full-time skilled nursing care, or speech or physical therapy. Note that the care provider has to be Medicare certified; it can't be your sister or neighbor. So in the same way that Medicare pays for only very few nursing home stays, the same is also true for home care.

Q. Are there any nursing services that Medicare will pay?

A. Don't faint, but yes, they will step in and pay a substantial portion if you should happen to need *hospice care*. Hospice care is given when a person is terminally ill and no recovery is expected. The caregiver is there simply to ease the pain and suffering of the patient and his or her family during the last days. Whether the services are provided in your own home or another facility does not matter.

Q. My mom is in an adult day-care center. Would Medicare cover the cost of this?

A. No. Remember, one of the requirements for Medicare paying is skilled care, not just custodial care.

As you can see, there are very few forms of continuing care that Medicare will pay anything for. If this is a concern of yours, it is far wiser to make sure that you are covered with private long-term-care insurance.

LONG-TERM-CARE INSURANCE

Think of all the insurance that we carry on ourselves to protect us from things we hope will never happen, and that most of the time don't happen—fires, car theft, floods. Almost everybody who owns a home or a car has that kind of insurance. But there is one kind of insurance that most people do *not* have, yet they are more likely to need it than any of those other policies. This is insurance for long-term care in a nursing home.

Please keep an open mind when reading this section. You might think, "*I* will never end up in a nursing home." I assure you, that is exactly what all the people who are in nursing homes today thought as well. Every client I have ever talked to knows people who have been wiped clean of every cent they had because of the costs of nursing home care. In my opinion, this is one of the most important insurance policies you can have, especially if you are married. You may feel you're too young to think about this now. Well, if you are fifty or older, you should be thinking about it now. If you are not yet fifty, keep this book handy, for one day you will be, and then you can use it to help you ask and answer some of the questions that you may have. The following questions will give you an idea of the most important things to know about long-term-care (LTC) insurance.

Q. I already have health insurance. Why do I need long-term-care insurance?

A. For a very good reason. There is not one health insurance policy available today that will cover a long-term-care stay. That's right: If you end up in a nursing home (and statistics say that after the age of sixty-five one out of three of you reading this book will spend some time during your life in a nursing home), your health insurance is not going to pay for it. As you have seen in the previous sections,

Medicare will not pay for it, you don't want to have to go on Medicaid, nor will Medigap policies pay. If you do not have long-term-care insurance, you will be the one responsible for all the costs—and they can be enormous.

Q. Insurance agents are always calling me up to try to sell me long-term-care insurance. How do I know if I should buy it?

A. There are many questions you have to ask yourself. The first question before you buy anything is, "Can I afford it?" Of course the agents want you to buy a policy, that's how they make their living, but I am more concerned about you than them. With LTC insurance, you have to know if you can afford it not only today, but ten years from now, twenty years, thirty years, and forty years from now. The average age of entry into a nursing home is eighty-four. If you've just turned fifty, you may not use this policy for thirty or forty years. Imagine you get a great policy, you pay your premiums every year for the next twenty-five years. Now imagine that at age seventy-five you find that you cannot afford to pay the premiums anymore. All those years of paying will have been for nothing, for as soon as you stop paying the premiums, most policies are dead. In essence you've made a donation to your insurance company. You paid them good money for a number of years and they never had to pay out a cent. You would have done better to blow the money in Las Vegas—at least you would have had a good time out of it. (There are some policies that allow you to get money back if you drop the policy, but these often aren't worth it—see the next question.)

Seriously, you must give careful consideration to your future cash flow. So project out into the distant future, when maybe your spouse has died and your pension and Social Security income is cut in half—look into all the possibilities and calculate, realistically, if you will always be able to afford the monthly premiums without a shadow of a doubt. If the answer is no, then you would be better off in most cases to take the money you have now and, instead of putting it toward LTC premiums, start investing it on your own in case a need for long-term care strikes your family one day. I would also immediately seek the advice of an elder care lawyer to see how you can protect what you have.

If you're sure you can afford the premiums, the next question is, What's the worst-case scenario of what could happen if you did not have long-term-care insurance? Maybe you are single with no children and really have very little money. If this is your situation, in the worst-case scenario you most likely would qualify eventually for Medicaid, and maybe you should just tell those insurance agents to stop calling you. Again, before you commit to anything, see if you can find a professional who can advise you and tell you for sure if this is the right decision. If you want, you can always call me and I will help you. In fact, I urge you to do so before you do buy a policy. Sometimes a little knowledge is a dangerous thing, so let's make sure you are doing what's right.

If you are married, then LTC insurance becomes far more important. There is nothing more devastating than to watch a healthy at-home husband spend every last penny on his wife in the nursing home (or vice versa) and have nothing left to live on at all. *It happens all the time,* so please do not think this is an area not to pay attention to. If they can afford it, I would highly recommend that the majority of married couples make seriously looking into long-term-care insurance a real priority. Make those agents who keep calling you educate you on this topic, and compare closely all the policies out there, and soon it will become clear which one to buy. My books *The 9 Steps to Financial Freedom* and *You've Earned It, Don't Lose It* cover this subject in more depth, including all the questions you must ask about LTC policies.

Q. Should I buy a policy that will give me back everything I paid into it if I don't use it or if I drop the policy after a number of years?

A. This is a *return-of-premium policy.* I'm still as of this writing not a big fan of these policies, and here's why: For the privilege of being able to get your money back, the insurance company charges you 35 percent a year more than what your premiums would be without that feature. Usually if you read the small print, you will see that you have to pay into these policies for a minimum of ten to twenty years before they will pay you back 100 percent of what you paid in. If you bought an excellent policy at age fifty-eight and were in good health when you did so, your premium would be about $1,000 a year without the return-of-premium feature, and $1,350 a year with it, a difference of $350. If you invested that $350 a year for the next twenty years and were able to get a 10 percent rate of return on that money, you would have about $20,000 saved at the end of that time—exactly the same amount that you would have in the policy if you had been paying the $1,000 a year. You see, in this case you could use the policy and still have that extra $20,000 in the bank. This is why I do not like most return-of-premium policies, but there are always exceptions to the rule, so you simply have to do the math. The numbers will tell you which is the best way to go.

Q. My agent who keeps calling me to sell me a policy represents only one company. You have said on QVC that it is very important to make sure that your agent can sell you a policy from a number of different companies. Why is this?

A. Whether it's long-term-care insurance or any other kind, for that matter, when an agent can sell you a policy from only one particular company, he or she is known as a *captured agent,* meaning that the agent is not necessarily free to sell you the best policy that money can buy. It is not that agents don't want to do so, it's that they are not permitted to do so. Agents who are free to sell you any and all policies can talk to you about the pros and cons of each one and offer you what they believe is the best policy. Even if you are dealing with an agent who can offer you many policies, you should still shop around, for you want to make sure that the one they offer is the best policy for you, not just the one that pays the highest commissions.

Q. Is it true that long-term-care insurance is now tax-deductible?

A. The answer is, "Sort of." As an individual you will be able to deduct a portion of premiums in the same way you deduct your other medical expenses, but for most of you that means you will not be able to deduct it at all. This is because on your income tax form you can deduct only medical expenses that are greater than 7.5 percent of your adjusted gross income. So if you have an adjusted gross income of $32,000, and you have medical expenses that are greater than $2,400, you can take those expenses and some of the premiums of your long-term-care insurance premium off your taxes. If, however, you do not exceed that 7.5 percent figure, then you don't get to deduct anything.

Q. My company is offering a group LTC insurance plan. Should I sign up for it?

A. Many group plans, believe it or not, may be not as good as an individual policy that you can get on your own. Check out the cost and benefits to an individual plan and then compare them to your group plan, and the answer will be very easy for you. Some good companies to compare your group plan against are CNA (which is my favorite), John Hancock, UNUM, Travelers, and GE Capital.

Q. My next-door neighbor just bought a long-term-care policy and told me that the best way to save money on a policy is to get the highest elimination period possible. Is this correct?

A. Neighbors are great for giving you a cup of sugar when you run out, but they're not so great for giving you financial advice. For those of you who don't know the term, the *elimination period* is the length of time before your policy will start to pay if you go into a nursing home—that is, the number of days you have to pay out of your own pocket. If you are admitted into a nursing home and you have a ninety-day elimination period in your LTC policy, you will have to pay for the first ninety days yourself. If you have a zero-day elimination period, the policy will pay from the very first day you are admitted.

Of course a policy with a higher elimination period is less expensive than one with a low elimination period at first look, but the real savings is quite small in comparison to what the cheaper policy could end up costing you. For instance, a great policy for someone fifty-nine years of age in perfect health with a zero-day elimination period will cost $1,255 a year every year from that point on, as long as the company does not have an across-the-board premium hike. If you were to get the exact same policy but with a thirty-day elimination, it would cost you $1,187, or only $68 less per year. A ninety-day elimination period would cost $1,118 per year, or $137 less than the zero-day. But what if you need to use this policy? Since the average age of entry into a nursing home is eighty-four, and in this example the person is fifty-nine, that gives us twenty-six years before we most likely will need to use this policy. Twenty-six years from now, the average monthly cost of a nursing home is projected to be $11,000 to $30,000, depending on where you live. If you had gotten a thirty-day elimination period, you would have to come up with this $11,000 to $30,000 out of your own pocket. If you had gotten the ninety-day elimination, you might be forking out anywhere from $30,000 to $90,000 for those ninety days. I would much rather pay $137 more per year, which is less than $12 a month, than tens of thousands of dollars sometime in the future.

Sometimes when you pay less, you may end up paying a whole lot more. So as you can see, the answer to this question is a resounding NO.

Q. I have no idea as to how much an LTC policy costs. Can you give me an idea?

A. For everyone, it will depend on the insurance company you choose as well as your age, your health, and what benefits you select. But just to give you an idea, here are some prices from a company by the name of CNA. These quotes assume that the person is in great health and that the benefits are as follows.

⇥ A lifetime benefit period, which means that this policy will pay for as long as you are in a nursing home, for your whole lifetime.

⇥ A benefit amount of $100 a day. This is how much starting today the policy will pay per day toward your nursing home.

⇥ An inflation rider of 5 percent compounded. This means that the benefit amount will increase each year for the rest of the time the policy is in force by 5 percent compounded. So in thirty years, that $100 a day will have grown to $412 a day to keep up with the rising costs of nursing homes. This policy will also include $50 a day with 5 percent compound inflation for two years of home health care as well.

For a policy with all these benefits, which right now is one of the very best available, the costs are as follows (varying slightly depending on your state of residence).

AGE WHEN POLICY IS TAKEN OUT	PREMIUM (PER YEAR)
50–54	$954
55–59	$1,255
60–64	$1,719
65	$2,580
70	$3,723
75	$6,734

If you think about it, you will see that the amount of money that you will spend for the entire time that you have this policy will be less than just a few months in a nursing home. If you buy a policy when you are fifty-nine and enter a nursing home at the age of eighty-four, you will have spent $24,804 ($954 × 26) for the LTC policy—far less than what a few months in a nursing home will cost you.

EARLY RETIREMENT AND RETIREMENT ACCOUNTS

I cannot tell you the number of questions I get about early retirement and retirement accounts. It is interesting to think that most of us will spend more years in retirement than we ever did working, now that we are all living into our late eighties and early nineties. If you are not at retirement age yet, read these questions anyway, for some of these issues are ones to think about years before you actually retire. And in today's economy, retirement may come sooner than you expected. . . .

Q. I have just been offered early retirement with a severance package at work which I want to take. Can I also qualify for unemployment?

A. If your early retirement is offered via a severance package, most likely you will qualify for unemployment to help you out for a while. In many cases, even if your early retirement is on a voluntary basis, you can still qualify for unemployment. Recently I was consulting for a large company where they offered early retirement to the management sector. Many of these managers applied and qualified for unemployment. If you are taking early retirement and your job is being eliminated, try to get a letter from the company stating this. It will help you if you apply for unemployment. Even if you cannot get a letter, it's worth giving it a good try.

Q. With my early retirement offer from the company that I am working for, I will no longer have dental insurance. The company is offering me the chance to continue my dental insurance with them if I pay for it under a program known as COBRA. Should I take it for my wife and myself?

A. A dental plan for COBRA may cost a husband and wife $58 a month. Besides paying this premium, you would also have to pay approximately 20 percent or more of the cost of any work you have done. Suppose that during the year you and your spouse have two teeth cleanings each at a cost of $50 each, and you each have a set of X rays for $80 each, and your spouse has a crown replaced for $350. All this would total $710. If you had chosen to insure yourself under COBRA to pay for these costs, it would have cost you $58 a month, or $696 and 20 percent of the $710, or $142, for a total of $838—$128 more than if you had just paid for it out of your own pocket. The rule of thumb is, if you think you will need more than $900 a year of work, take advantage of COBRA; otherwise, put about $60 a month away to cover dental expenses for when they arise.

Q. I'm taking early retirement, and I have a nice chunk of change in my 401(k) at work. I have been told that I can transfer this money to an IRA rollover. What is that?

A. It is a means of transferring assets from one tax-deferred retirement fund, such as your company's qualified plan, to another tax-deferred account. You do this by "rolling it over" into another tax-deferred account—held in your name at a bank or financial institution, known as an IRA rollover.

Q. What are my tax consequences?

A. None at the time of transfer. When you withdraw your funds, you will be taxed on the amount withdrawn as ordinary income in the year of withdrawal.

Q. Can I withdraw my money at any time in an IRA rollover?

A. You may not withdraw your funds prior to the age of 59½. If you do, you will be assessed a 10 percent penalty on the amount of funds withdrawn.

Q. How long can I leave my funds in an IRA rollover?

A. By April 1 of the year after you have turned 70½, you must have started withdrawing your funds in whatever amount you like as long as you take out the minimum requirement. If the minimum is not withdrawn, a 50 percent penalty will be charged on the amount that you should have withdrawn.

Q. If I am still employed at the age of 70½, do I have to take money out of my 401(k)?

A. No. If the money is in an employer's qualified retirement plan, such as a 401(k), you do not have to start making withdrawals until you actually retire.

Q. If I retire at the age of seventy-five, when do I have to start taking my money out of my 401(k)?

A. By April 1 of the year after you have turned seventy-five, or whatever age you may happen to be when you really retire.

Q. Is it the same for IRA rollovers? If I am still working at the age of 70½, do I have to withdraw my money from my IRA rollover?

A. YES. *The rules that govern IRA rollovers and the rules that govern 401(k)s and other employer-sponsored retirement plans are different.*

Q. When I asked about taking money out of my 401(k), I was told that they would withhold 20 percent. Why?

A. From any amount of money that is distributed directly from your employer-sponsored retirement account to you, your company has to withhold 20 percent. This is an IRS rule. You owe taxes on that money, and the IRS wants it as soon as you withdraw it. So if you withdraw $10,000, you will receive only $8,000. The company has to withhold 20 percent, or $2,000 in this case, for taxes, just as they withhold taxes from your paycheck. This IRS rule *does not* apply to withdrawals from an IRA.

Q. If I am transferring this money from my 401(k) to my IRA rollover, will the company still withhold the 20 percent?

A. No. When the company transfers your funds directly from your qualified retirement account to an IRA rollover, then no tax is withheld. The 20 percent penalty is only withheld on funds distributed and made payable to you from your qualified retirement account.

Q. How long do I have before I have to roll over my funds?

If you have your company send you the money directly (which is not recommended), you have sixty days from the day you receive your distribution to roll that money over into an IRA rollover. If you fail to do so, you will be taxed on the entire amount of the distribution.

Q. Where can I open up an IRA rollover?

A. You can open IRA rollovers at banks, insurance companies, brokerage firms, discount brokerage firms, mutual funds companies, and credit unions.

Q. I am fifty-six and my company has just handed me the pink slip. The only way for me and my family to make it is to start taking money out of our 401(k) plan. Is there anything I can do to avoid the 10 percent federal tax penalty if I withdraw this money?

A. Yes, as a matter of fact there is. Read closely, for this is one of the best-kept secrets in town. If you are fifty-five or older in the year of retirement, then you can withdraw any money you want *from a 401(k)* without having to pay that 10 percent federal tax penalty. They will withhold the 20 percent tax I just mentioned, but who cares? You would have had to pay taxes on that money sooner or later anyway.

Q. If I have moved my money to an IRA rollover and I have retired at the age of fifty-five or older, can I still take this money out without penalty in any amount that I so desire?

A. NO! The fifty-five or older rule *only applies to employer-sponsored retirement plans like the 401(k)*. If you roll your money over to an IRA, this rule does not apply to you anymore.

Q. Can I roll over part of my distribution and keep some in the 401(k)?

A. Yes.

Q. Is there a way to get money out of my IRA rollover prior to the age of 59½ without having to pay that 10 percent penalty?

A. Yes. The wisest way is under a system known as Substantially Equal Periodic Payments. This is where you would choose an amount of money that you would have to take out of your IRA rollover every single year for the next five years or until you turn 59½, whichever is longer. So if you start making withdrawals when you are 52, you have to take out the predecided amount every year until you're 59½, or for seven years. If you're 56 when you start, you have to take the money out until you're 62, for remember it is 59½ or five years, whichever is longer. In this case five years is longer. For more detailed information, you can see my book *You've Earned It, Don't Lose It.* Also please make sure that you see a tax adviser before you make any moves that involve your retirement.

COLLEGE TUITION AND FINANCIAL AID

One of the largest expenses that most families have is the financing of a college education. To help make this dream a reality, some people even start investing before their baby is born. Nonetheless, a lot of us will still need financial aid to help us out. Here are some of the questions that I've been asked about how to save, what to invest in, and what you need to know about financial aid for your children's college education.

Q. I have been thinking about getting one of the prepaid tuition plans that are offered in my state to help pay for my child's college education. Do you think this is a good idea?

A. Maybe yes and maybe no. They can be great for a few people: those who are in a high tax bracket (since the earnings are tax-deferred), or those who are only comfortable investing their money in something like a passbook savings account.

If you have what it takes to invest in a good no-load mutual growth fund and/or stocks, you most likely will come out with far more cash than you would with a prepaid plan. This is especially true, since the rise in the cost of education has been pulling back from that annual 6 percent increase that we have grown accustomed to. With the prepaid plans, you win if the costs of schools rise faster than the annual rate of return you can get from your other investments, and you lose if it doesn't.

There is one other major reservation I have about these tuition plans, even though I know they are the talk of the town. For these plans to be of value, the following two things have to happen: Number one, when your children get to the college age, they have to decide they actually want to go—and guess what, their idea of what they want to do with their life, especially at seventeen or eighteen, may not be the same as what you think they ought to do. Number two, not only do they have to want to go to college, but they have to want to go to one of the state schools that you have committed to via this prepaid tuition plan. If they want to go out of state to a different school, you may not be so happy that you have one of these plans. Another thing to be very careful of is that with most schools, if you have a prepaid tuition plan, it can knock you out of the running for financial aid. For all these reasons I'm currently not a great advocate of prepaid plans.

Q. My broker told me that the best way to fund my new-born boy's education is by investing my money within a uniform gift to minors account. Is this true?

A. Again, maybe yes and maybe no. The main reason that most people use a UGMA account is that, depending on what you invest in it, there can be some savings to you in how this money is taxed. I do not think the tax advantages are worth giving up ownership of this money and this is why: If you start investing now while your boy is still just a few months old, depending on how much you put away and what you invest it in, you could have a sizable sum of money when he turns eighteen. But there is no way to be certain that your little Johnny Angel is going to grow up to be as sweet or as wonderful as he is right now. And when you place money in an account under the uniform gift to minors account, *you have given your child an irrevocable gift.* By law, when that kid turns eighteen, he is entitled to that money, and can spend it any way his little eighteen-year-old heart wants to. Over the years I have seen many UGMA accounts that were supposed to fund college educations go instead to funding the latest in cars or to support a drug or alcohol habit while Mom and Pop had to watch brokenhearted, with nothing they could do about it.

I always advise that if in fact you want to put money aside for your kid's education, you do so—but keep it in a separate account in your name. By the way, in regard to taxes, if you invest in a good growth-oriented investment such as stocks or stock mutual funds, and if you hold them for the long haul, the increase will most likely qualify as a capital gain, which reduces the taxes to be paid over the years anyway. So even the tax advantage of a UGMA may be less than it first appears.

Q. I've heard it'll be easier for my daughter to qualify for college financial aid if the money is in a UGMA account. Isn't that a consideration?

A. This, too, depends on your individual situation, but here's what you need to know. When you apply for financial aid, the college will expect you to contribute the money that you have in your name at the rate of 6 percent, while they'll take 35 percent of the money your daughter has in hers. Say you have assets of $30,000 in your name and the tuition of the school that your daughter wants to go to is $8,000 a year. They will take 6 percent of that $30,000, or $1,800. The rest could possibly be paid for with some help from financial aid. If you had that same $30,000 in a UGMA account, they will expect you to use these funds at the rate of 35 percent, or $10,500. That's a big difference! Think about paying $10,500 from a UGMA account rather than $1,800 from your account, and tell me if a UGMA account makes sense if you are applying for financial aid.

I don't think so.

Q. My daughter, who is now twenty-seven, finally decided that now she is ready to go to college and we will need to apply for financial aid. She currently does not live at home. Should she move back home before she applies for financial aid?

A. This one may depend on which school she is going to go to. But generally, in order for her to be considered an independent student and to qualify for financial aid based on her finances alone, your daughter will have had to live on her own for two to three years, and you must not have claimed her on your tax return for those years. If your child is under twenty-four years of age, regardless of where she lives, your assets will be counted toward financial aid. So be careful and check it out with a financial adviser at the school you are considering.

Q. What do you think is the best way to invest money to finance a child's education?

A. I believe stocks, especially in the form of mutual funds, if you are a novice, are the best way to invest for long-term growth. However, anytime you're considering an investment, *how soon you will have to actually use that money* is critical to choosing investment placement. I personally like to see a minimum of ten years when one invests in stocks or mutual growth funds. The reason for this is that there has never been a ten-year period of time, regardless of the day that you invested, that the stock market has not outperformed every other investment out there. Even if you had invested all your money in the market the day before the crash of 1987, if you had just left your money alone, you could have taken it out ten years later and made an excellent return. This has always been true when you look back throughout history.

In the shorter term, the ups and downs of stocks could be a problem. If you have only a few years, say two or three, till your kid will be going to school, then you have to be quite careful. What you *don't* want to have happen is to invest that money for growth, by buying a good mutual growth fund for example, and in a sudden downturn of the market, lose not only all your gains but some of the principal, just before you need this money. If you're going to need money in just two to five years, I would stay conservative with your investments by keeping the money in high-yielding money-market funds, or Treasury notes, CDs, series EE bonds, and investments like that. If you're somewhere in between—say, you have six or seven years before you'll have to lay hands on the cash, you might still consider investing for growth if you feel comfortable doing so. One of my favorite places to invest for a low-maintenance good-return investment is a Standard & Poor's 500 index fund. Several houses offer them; the one that I like the best is offered by Vanguard Mutual Funds.

However, let me make a disclaimer right here and now. Since I have not met you personally and do not know other extremely pertinent factors, such as how you feel about investing, your level of sophistication, your total financial situation, I would suggest that you seek professional advice from someone who can help you construct a sensible financial profile, or that you do significant research on your own before you actually invest this money. Investing is far more than just taking a sum of money and plunking it somewhere. It is watching your money, and most of all making sure that wherever you put it makes you feel powerful. (See chapter 6 of *The 9 Steps to Financial Freedom* for more on this.)

I hope this will at least give you an idea of how to start.

Q. Do college financial-aid applications require both parents to list income, assets, etc.? I am divorced and solely responsible for my children's education, but I'm afraid I won't qualify for financial aid if their father's income is considered.

A. Twenty-seven percent of all financial-aid applicants come from divorced families, so this is a common problem. Financial aid is complicated enough, and divorce makes it only more so. Schools want to know about the finances of both parents, and remarried parents need to detail the finances of their new spouses as well. Most schools, however, will take a look at your situation and will make case-by-case decisions.

This is often a relationship issue even more than a financial issue. Try to make sure that both you and your spouse do what's appropriate for the children, and that paying for college, or not paying, does not become a way of getting back at your ex.

Q. Where can I find information about grants as well as financial aid?

A. There are some great sources of information on the Internet, which you can get access to in most public libraries if you don't have a computer at home. Check out FastWEB, a scholarship search engine that lets Internet users search, without cost, a database of more than 180,000 private scholarships.

For more general information on college financing, check out *The A's and B's of Academic Scholarships* (Octameron, $7) and *College Financial Aid* (Arco, $22). For more information on campus moneymaking opportunities, see *College Checkmate: Innovative Tuition Plans That Make You a Winner* (Octameron, $7).

CREDIT CARDS AND DEBT

For most of us, debt is a major part of our financial lives. With the thousands of credit card offers being thrown before us, one would almost have to be as great as Houdini to be able to escape the temptation to get into debt.

But once you're in debt, it's like a black hole that even Houdini would have a hard time getting out of. Even if we have good credit, we can still have problems with unscrupulous credit card companies. So read the questions below—I'm sure there will be ones that you can relate to.

Q. I know I have good credit, but in search of a better interest rate, I just applied to five of those low-cost credit cards and I was turned down on all of them. How is that possible?

A. Whenever you apply for a credit card, that fact will automatically show on your credit report. When you apply to many companies at once, all the companies will see this activity and immediately come to the conclusion that you are about to go credit crazy and get into big-time debt, so it is quite possible that none of them will give you a card. It never dawns on these credit geniuses that you just may be simply shopping for the best deal in town, but there's nothing you can do about their policy.

You should wait at least six months before applying for a new card. During that time check the rates on several cards and pick one and only one card that you would like to have. Then apply to that card alone.

Q. Does it make sense to take a cash advance from one of these low-rate credit cards and invest that money in the market if I can make more than what the interest rate is costing me?

A. Please do not do this. It might work out just fine but it also could blow up in your face. *Never go into debt so you can invest*. When you think you can outsmart the markets is when you get into real trouble.

I know it sounds like a great idea. Borrow money at 5.9 percent, invest it in stocks or a mutual fund, and make 20 percent. But when you take a cash advance from one of these credit cards, it will not be at that low rate of, let's say, 5.9 percent. Most cash advances are at the highest interest rate a card company can charge, around 21 percent. So to be able to consistently get a 21 percent return on your money would make you the best investment adviser in the world. But just to go into a little more detail, let's say that you could borrow money at a decent rate and invest it in a stock or mutual fund and make 20 percent. You could get rich on borrowed money, right? But here's what could happen to you instead. The stock market's booming; you borrow this money and invest it. Then the market takes a turn and starts to go down. As you see money that is not yours to begin with start to bleed away, you're going to start worrying that you could lose it all. You end up selling and taking a loss, just a small one if you're lucky. Now you not only don't have that money but you have debt as well. The bottom line is, if you have to borrow to invest in the stock market, don't.

Q. I know I should be putting away savings for the future, but I'm also carrying a lot of credit card debt. Should I pay off the debt first before I start investing?

A. It will depend on how high the interest rate is on your credit card. You could think of it this way: if you're paying 18 percent on your credit card, that's like investing your money at minus 18 percent! If you invested, say, $1,000 and got a solid return of 10 percent on it over a year, but you carried $1,000 on your 18 percent card for the same time, you'll have made $100 on your investment but you'll owe another $180 in interest on your credit card. You made 10 percent with money that cost you 18 percent.

If your credit card interest is below 8 percent, then I would say that it is okay to save and pay off your credit cards over time. It is always good to get in the habit of saving, and the sooner you start investing for the future, the better. If the interest is above 8 percent, pay off your cards first. For that matter, if you are paying interest in the teens, you should really try to find a lower-rate card if you can get one. There are plenty of cards around with rates less than 10 percent.

Q. I have a $3,300 balance on a credit card that charges me 12 percent. I know there are lower-rate cards, but how much will I really save if I switch? Also, some people say you should pay more than the minimum amount each month, but that's so hard to do—my minimum is already about $100 a month! Does more make much of a difference?

A. Well, since the average credit card debt in the United States is about $4,000, I am sure that many people reading this will be able to relate to this question! The best way to answer your question is simply to let the numbers do the talking. At the 12 percent you are currently being charged:

Paying $100 a month, at the end you will have paid $725 in interest

Paying $150 a month, at the end you will have paid $446 in interest

Paying $200 a month, at the end you will have paid $324 in interest

If your balance is $3,300 and your card charges 5.9 percent:

Paying $100 a month, at the end you will have paid $309 in interest

Paying $150 a month, at the end you will have paid $201 in interest

CREDIT CARDS AND DEBT

Paying $200 a month, at the end you will have paid
    $150 in interest

You can see that every bit you can pay over the minimum will help reduce the actual interest amount consider-
ably. The interest cost on 12 percent is more than double
that of the 5.9 percent card. You will also see that the more
you pay monthly, the less you pay in interest. Lots less—
a little more goes a long way when it comes to credit
card debt.

**Q. How long does it take to remove my bad credit from
my credit report? And how do I know if it is has been
cleared?**

A. The credit reporting companies are supposed to remove
your bad credit listing after seven years, or ten years if it
was for a bankruptcy.
    The name of the three bureaus you want to make sure
clear your records are these:

TRW
PO Box 8030
Layton, UT 84041-8030
800-682-7654

Trans Union Corp.
PO Box 3307
Tampa, FL 33601
800-226-4550

Equifax Credit Information Services, Inc.
PO Box 105873
Atlanta, GA 30374-0256
800-685-1111
404-250-4100

Send or call for a report. It will be free if you have been turned down for credit in the past sixty days or if there is a dispute; otherwise, it will cost about eight dollars.

If you are still having trouble with credit after seven years, Bankcard Holders of America offers a helpful booklet, *Understanding Credit Bureaus,* for a dollar. Call them at 540-389-5445, or write 524 Branch Drive, Salem, VA 24153. They also offer for four dollars a list of credit cards with low interest rates once your credit is cleaned up, as well as cards that fit your situation. Call and talk to them. Take a look, too, at two nifty little books they publish: *Consumer Credit Rights* and *Getting Out of Debt.*

Q. I have been told that since I have bad credit I should try to find a secured credit card. Can you tell me what that is and where to find one?

A. Having a *secured credit card* means that you make a deposit into an account at a bank or other savings institution and they use that money to secure your credit line. If you fail to pay your credit card bill, they simply take the money that you owe them from your deposit. So it is your own money that is being offered as security against your getting into debt again.

If you need a credit card, you might just want to take the safe route and get a secured credit card. It may be less convenient than other cards, because the amount of your credit line will be limited to how much you have on deposit, but if you've had real trouble with credit card debt in the past this may be good for you.

Q. I got seriously behind in my payments to my credit card companies and they turned them over to a collection agency. Ever since then I have been fighting off collectors. I've been making small payments every month in an amount I can afford, but these collectors keep calling me day and night, even at my place of employment. I have told them I'm paying my debts to the best of my ability and asked them to stop harassing me, but this seems to do absolutely no good. Legally, how can I get these people to leave me alone and just accept the fact that I am making a consistent effort to pay off my debts according to what I can afford?

A. What you can do is to follow this advice from John Cioffi, author of *Protecting Your Credit*.

Make something very clear, a consumer should never have verbal dialogue with a collector under any circumstance! To consumers everywhere . . . NEVER CALL A COLLECTOR! WRITE TO THEM (return receipt) and tell them the following:

> "*As you know, Section 805a (1) states, 'Without the prior consent of a consumer given directly to the debt collector or the express permission of a court of competent jurisdiction, a debt collector may not communicate with a consumer in connection with the collection of any debt at any unusual time or place or at a time or place known or which should be known to be inconvenient to the consumer.' I am emphatically stating that at my place of work, my home, or anywhere else regarding this matter is inconvenient to me. Your failure to comply with this request will subject your organization to civil liability under the Fair Debt Collection Practices Act, Section 813, which is*

$500,000 or 1 percent of your net worth, whichever is less.

All dialogue from this moment on will be conducted through the U.S. Mail only."

Think about it! Once you have told them in writing (you should copy this letter word for word and send it to them), and have proof someone signed for this letter, that office is now on the hook to the FULLEST EXTENT OF THE LAW! Any collector, or any of its employees, who would be stupid enough to continue to make calls after you invoked your rights under federal law (the Fair Debt Collection Practices Act), has left that agency open to a lawsuit, which you will win easily! There have been several successfully instigated suits against collectors. In each case, no exceptions, the consumer has won in court or received a handsome settlement! If anyone has been called after invoking these rights, and has proof that they did, he or she should immediately seek a qualified attorney in this field.

Q. I've put myself into thousands of dollars of credit card debt. I have an IRA account that is invested in a great mutual fund. Should I take the money out of my IRA and pay off my credit card debt? I am fifty-three years old.

A. In my opinion it would not be wise to take the money from your IRA to pay off your credit card debt. Anyone under the age of fifty-nine and a half who withdraws money from a retirement account will have to pay a 10 percent federal tax penalty and a state tax penalty, and will also have to pay ordinary income tax on that money. At age fifty-three this will apply to you. So after you pay the penalty and the income tax on the funds you withdraw, you'll have only about 30 to 50 percent of what you took out. That is too high a price to pay in the majority of cases just to pay off credit card debt. Remember, too, that money is in your retirement account for you to live on when you are no longer working, and you'll need it then just as much as you think you need it now. So without taking money out of your IRA, try to start to eliminate that credit card debt slowly but surely. It may take you a few years to pay it down completely, but at the end of that time you will be very glad you still have that money in your IRA. To help you do this, please see *The 9 Steps to Financial Freedom.*

Q. If I'm married, am I responsible for money that my husband owes on credit cards that are in his name alone, and vice versa?

A. This depends on which state you live in. Often you are responsible for your spouse's debt whether or not your name is on the account. For instance, in California, a community-property state, if hubby goes out the day after you are married and gets a Visa card, charges $5,000 on it, and then cannot pay for it, guess who is also liable? So watch out: Having separate credit cards may not give you any protection. Check out the laws for your state.

Q. I'm deeply in debt and I'm thinking of claiming bankruptcy. What are the ramifications?

A. This is a very interesting question—for there are emotional ramifications as well as financial ones.

Bankruptcy is not something to be taken lightly. I consider it for my clients only after much thought and when and only when there is no other way out. Before you take such action, there are many questions that you must ask yourself. Filing for bankruptcy may help you with *your* money problems, but it doesn't help those to whom you owe that money. Think about how you'd feel if someone owed you a lot of money and you got a letter saying, "Sorry, I'm bankrupt, I won't be paying you back."

Think about whom you owe this money to. Credit cards? Friends? Businesses? Will you have to see these people after you claim bankruptcy, and if so, how will that make you feel? What financial hardship, if any, will you put others into if you take such an action? Why are you thinking about claiming bankruptcy? Is there absolutely no other way that you can climb out of debt little by little with work and effort—or are you just looking for a quick fix?

On the purely financial side, bankruptcy will stay on your record for ten years and cannot be removed prior to that time.

Whatever you decide about bankruptcy, my advice is to *remember how you got into this mess and how it feels,* and after you have solved this situation (which you will), let it always serve as a reminder for yourself and others that debt of any kind is bondage. Make sure *The 9 Steps to Financial Freedom* is your new best friend.

Q. If I claim bankruptcy, does that mean that I will not be able to get another credit card?

A. Years ago that is exactly what it would have meant. Nowadays, however, the credit card companies—always thinking creatively, it seems, for ways to get people in trouble—look at it differently. Some of these companies apparently look for people who have claimed bankruptcy and offer them credit cards. What's wrong with that? you may ask. Well, once you have claimed bankruptcy, you cannot do so again for seven years. Within that time, if you get into trouble on your credit cards, there is no way you can get out of paying those debts.

If you have been having trouble getting a credit card because you have bad credit, and have been afraid to claim bankruptcy because you were afraid you'd never get a card, think again. You may find it's easier to get the card after bankruptcy. But if it's your credit cards that got you into trouble in the first place, you are really playing with fire if you apply for a card again after bankruptcy.

Q. What is the difference between Chapter 7 bankruptcy and Chapter 13?

A. Very briefly, in Chapter 7, every debt you have is wiped out. In Chapter 13 bankruptcy, you are allowed to pay back your debts, usually at a discounted rate, over a period of time (maximum sixty months) without any additional interest accruing during that time. You should be aware that in a few states, legislation has been introduced to get rid of Chapter 7 because it has cost the credit card companies too much money.

Q. Is there anything I should look for in a credit card besides the lowest interest rate and no annual fee? Are there other things that I need to be aware of?

A. The card issuers are constantly coming up with subtle new ways to make money off their cardholders, and it's hard to keep up with them all. But here are a few things that you need to keep in mind. Ever since the yearly fees became so commonplace, the companies have found other ways to make it up. For instance, it used to be that if you were late with your payment, you'd have a grace period usually up to ten days. Now many of the companies will charge you if you are late by just one day. Also ask the companies how much they will charge you for being late—the fee is now typically around $20, which really adds up if you are late two or three times a year. (The companies don't mind giving up the annual fee if they can get several times that much out of you in late fees.)

Another thing you have to be careful of is going over your credit limit. Here is another catch-22 for most of us. You would think that the credit card companies would not let you spend more than your limit, and that if you did, your charge would be denied. On the contrary: They'll let you go over the limit, and charge you another $20 or so for the privilege. In the good old days, many of the credit card issuers allowed you to go over by up to 20 percent without charging you anything. Not anymore!

Finally, read the fine print on your cardholder agreement for one more important thing: If you are late with a payment or go over your limit, not only can the company charge you a fee; in many cases it can raise your interest rate dramatically. That's right, your sweet 5.9 percent could be in the 20s before you know it.

You should look for all these hidden and contingent charges as well as annual fees and interest rates. And by the way, about the interest rate on your card, you should ask not only how much it is but how the company computes it. Many of the companies are now compounding this interest charge daily on your balance rather than monthly, and this can make a significant difference. Sometimes I think we should call them "Halloween cards" instead of credit cards, for we really have no idea anymore if what we are getting is a treat or a trick.

Q. My credit card company just raised my interest rate for no reason at all. Can they do this?

A. Believe it or not, they probably can. When dealing with credit card companies, as a consumer you're usually in the position of "like it or lump it." It may be possible to lodge a complaint against the card company, but most likely you would have to go through a procedure called arbitration, which could end up costing you more than it would be worth.

Q. I always pay my bills on time and in full and now my credit card company is starting to charge me an annual fee. It seems as if I am getting penalized for being a good customer. Is this true?

A. Well, being a good customer so to speak is not what the companies want. Not that you should really care. You see, for the companies to keep you on their books, to send out your monthly statement, answer your calls, etc., it costs them about $20 a year. There are two ways they make this money back. Either by the interest that they charge you on your balance if you have one, or by the fees that the merchants have to pay them every time you use your card. So, if you carry an average balance of about $400 on even a low-interest rate card of 7.9 percent, they make money on you. If you spend about $3,000 a year in the stores, they also make money on you from the fees from the merchants. The higher the interest rate, the lower the balance you need to keep for them not to charge you that annual fee. So do not be surprised that if you do not spend a lot of money on your card and if you pay it off monthly, that they will very shortly hit you with a yearly fee. The bottom line is that they are in this business to make money and the more unhealthy you are with your spending habits, the more money they will make off of you. I say, help put them out of business and get out and stay out of debt. The time has come where we go back to checks and cash or using debit cards that take the money directly out of our account.

RELATIONSHIPS AND MONEY

It's hard enough to manage money on our own. Managing it with another person can be really complicated—not to mention that dealing with that person *about* money can be complicated, too. Here are some questions that many people who are in relationships, either married or just living together, have asked.

Q. My husband is a chronic spender, but whenever I try to talk to him about this, he says he only buys "necessities." We have built up a lot of debt because of this. I have a secret savings account but I am afraid if I use it to pay off the debts he will just run them up again. He also insists that he be the one to pay the bills—then he always pays them late, which is now ruining my credit as well! What can I do?

A. Until someone is willing to change, wants to change, and sees why they must change, they usually do not change. Did you know his spending habits before you married him? If so, what did you think? Money habits are just as hard to break as any drug habit or smoking habit or drinking habit. And it should be treated very much the same way. With tenderness yet directness.

So, for your own piece of mind, you have to have a heart-to-heart talk with your husband about your fears and your thoughts, *without accusing him of anything*. You might suggest that you take over the bill paying because it really upsets you when the bills are late. If he is not willing to have you do this, then ask him to promise you that he will pay those bills on time. He must agree that the first time he breaks that promise, from then on all bills will be paid by you. Anything that you agree on has to be put down in writing so that you both are clear that you have committed to the same things and then both of you have to sign it and keep a copy of it. When it comes to money, it is best to have everything in writing. This may save a lot of confusion and argument in the future.

As for his debt and spending, try to set up a time that you and he can go over the last year's financial information of all the credit card statements and checks (his and yours) for your household. Remember, you are doing this with the intent of managing your cash flow as a unit—*not* to catch him and say, "I told you, you spend too much money," but to see where your money is really going.

Together, go through every charge one by one and keep a running record of everything that was bought and for how much on a separate piece of paper. (See *The 9 Steps to Financial Freedom* for more detail.) When you have finished, add everything up. This process alone can be very revealing in regard to one's spending habits and could be the eye-opener that you both need. If it is (and you will be able to tell by both of your reactions), then you might decide to start being a real team and take some of your savings and clear up the debt that has been created. *You should agree to do this only if all credit cards are ripped up first.* I do not care how much control anyone believes he has over his spending, credit card debt will build itself back up if those cards are there to tempt him.

If you feel you must have a charge card for emergencies, get one like an American Express card, which has to be paid off each month, or get a debit Visa card that takes the money directly out of your savings account as you use it, or a secured card that asks you to deposit a sum of money to secure the line of credit. Again, put this agreement in writing.

This is a good place to start. If he is not open to doing any of this, then I am afraid you have serious problems, and you may want to seek the help of a professional. Being able to talk honestly and openly about money is essential for a relationship to work.

Q. I am about to get married after four years of being engaged. From day one I have wanted my husband-to-be to sign a prenuptial agreement but have been too afraid to say anything about it to him. I am tempted just to drop the whole idea, but every time I think I have, it keeps popping back into my head. What should I do?

A. The problem here is not that you wanted your fiancé to sign this agreement, but that you have waited four years to ask him to do so. This is a very sensitive topic for most couples. The topic of prenuptial agreements, whether you want to have one or want not to have one, needs to be talked about as soon as you think there is a real possibility that your relationship is here to stay. If the relationship does last and you decide to join households, that is when you should act on the discussion and have a prenuptial actually drawn up. When people wait to mention it, they make it very difficult on both parties. There's an implication that something has changed between the two of you if you suddenly bring the subject up on the eve of your wedding.

Isn't it strange that we are about to walk into the twenty-first century carrying eighteenth-century ideas about our money? Those ancient notions mess up not only our relationships with money, but with each other as well. I happen to think that signing a "prenup" is a great idea. This is simply a financial document that says whatever you came into this relationship with, you will get to leave with. Should that be a big deal?

Here is some advice about having a prenuptial agreement drawn up: Make sure that you each consult a lawyer—not the same one—to make sure that the final agreement works for both of you. This may feel a little strange, but it is best for you to each have separate representation. That way, if the agreement should ever come into play, neither of you can say that you did not know what you were signing or did not understand it. You should have the lawyers sign the agreement as well, to show that they both have reviewed it.

Remember that making up this kind of agreement is an act of love and respect, not one of pessimism or suspicion. So many people are hurt by the idea that this document means their partner doesn't trust them. In my experience that's not true. All of my clients who have wanted a prenuptial agreement have been motivated out of love and respect for their own and their partner's money and security, not out of disrespect or lack of trust. Furthermore, if I think of couples I've worked with in which the partners did not mind signing a prenuptial and in fact were happy to do so, not only are those couples still together today, but many of them have actually asked years afterward for the prenuptial to be rescinded. For those in which one partner opposed the idea from the start, the exact opposite is true: most of them ended up either separated or divorced.

My advice is to do it from the very beginning; let your beloved know that this is something that you believe in and that it is important to you. For if someone really loves you, he or she will want you to be protected and to feel safe, and should be more than happy to say not just "I do," but also "I'll sign."

Q. My husband passed away very unexpectedly, and now I am dealing with money for the first time ever. Our stockbroker wants me to make a lot of changes to the portfolio and immediately invest the life-insurance proceeds in the market, but I'm not sure I feel comfortable with that. What should I do?

A. When we lose someone we love, our body, mind, and spirit all go into a state of shock. That is not the time to make decisions with your money. We all deal with loss in our own way, but regardless of how we deal with it, it is not the time to be dealing with money, especially if you have not done so before. So put your insurance proceeds into a money-market account, or anywhere that you feel it will be safe. Leave the money there until you are more emotionally stable, so you can intelligently decide what to do with it; this usually takes about one year.

With other funds that you may have, go to see a financial professional, someone who comes *highly recommended,* and makes you feel from the second you walk in their door that they have your best interests at heart. Tell them you just want to make sure you are safe and sound for now and that you do not want to make any major commitments unless he or she feels that you need to. If they are good, they will tell you this without your even having to say anything. Discuss your situation in regard to your income, and whether you will need to make any adjustments not only in your portfolio, but in your lifestyle as well.

The most important thing to remember is that when you have just suffered a loss, it's not the time to start learning about money. When you are in a marriage or other close relationship, it is *vital,* and I cannot stress this enough, that both of you know everything there is to know about your money. Not only how to spend it, but how to invest it and why. Both of you should know where all the important documents are, and should know the answer to this question: If one of you were to die, is there enough income for the other person to be financially secure? Please ask this question while your partner is still around to be able to answer it. Little by little, step by step, you can and must learn to handle your money and make decisions that will be right for you in the long run.

Q. My boyfriend and I are about to move in together and probably will get married. Should we merge our money, or keep separate accounts?

A. You wouldn't give up your identity for your boyfriend, would you? Then why consider giving up your financial identity? Your money is an integral part of you, just as your boyfriend's money is an integral part of him. When you marry or live together, you're simply creating a new, third entity—a partnership—that deserves a bank account of its own. The answer is that you'll want to keep separate accounts, and you may also want to merge some of your money. What I've seen in my practice is that both partners have to be as committed financially as they are emotionally for the relationship to work, now and also in the future.

Keep separate accounts for your separate or personal expenses. You each have a right to a certain amount of autonomy when it comes to your money, and the right to decide how and when to spend the money you've earned, at least some of it. Keep separate credit cards as well, so as to establish your own financial identity in the world of credit, now and for whenever you may want it later. The next step is to open a third, joint account, to pay for joint expenses and to invest in your future together. Money going out can make anyone nervous; money coming in and growing is the way to nurture and share in tomorrow's fortunes together.

For as little as $1,000, you can open a money-market account together with a good mutual funds company, tap into it every month for your joint expenses, and also invest other sums of money so they can begin to grow. These accounts pay higher interest rates than savings accounts, and you can also write checks against them. (Some money-market accounts that are currently performing well are the E Fund, 800-223-7010; Aetna A, 800-367-7732; and Transamerica Premier, 800-892-7587.)

Let's say your joint expenses will be $3,000 a month. Based on what you make now, you've agreed that he will kick in $2,000 a month, and your share will be $1,500 a month. Of that total, $3,500, use $3,000 to pay your bills and $500 to invest for the future. Since you're both contributing all you can, in good faith you should share equally, not proportional to what you put in, in the abundance that will follow—that is, the future growth of that $500 per month. You're partners, after all, and you should have a stake in each other's future, not just this month's bills.

Money takes time to make, it needs time to grow, and it requires time to negotiate. The "M" discussion is not something you have just once. The more you talk about money—best-case scenarios, worst-case scenarios, likeliest-case scenarios—the easier it becomes to talk about. Money is always an issue in a relationship whether you realize it or not. Talking about money, and making sure both of you agree about how you deal with it, will make your relationship stronger.

Q. My partner and I have lived together for about three years now and I have supported her during that time. My income is quite high in comparison to hers at this moment. It seems as if this discrepancy in incomes has created a huge chasm between us. She feels as if she will never be able to keep up with me, so what is the point? How can I level the playing fields without having to give her up or my much-loved income?

A. Different salary levels can be extremely difficult when it comes to a relationship, but they don't have to be. Money can be one of the most creative forces as well as one of the most destructive, but one thing is for sure, it will always be a force that we will have to deal with.

Most couples think they have problems with money for the following reasons: one spends too much, the other refuses to spend at all; one refuses to deal with it, the other deals only with it; one couldn't care less about it, the other only cares about it; one has too much, and the other has too little. Sounds familiar?

The truth, however, is that our so-called money problems really have very little to do with money itself. They have to do with how our own self-worth compares to our net worth. We have been taught to judge our worth by how much we have in the bank, what clothes we wear or what cars we drive, which schools we can send our kids to, our job titles, and so on—and not by our thoughts, feelings, and deeds. It seems as if we value the financial result of our actions more than the actions themselves and their effects on other people.

Therefore, when someone has less money or simpler possessions than those around her—especially compared to the other person within her own relationship—she's likely to feel there's a chasm between her and her partner. It is said that the hardest thing to do in life is to jump a chasm in two leaps. If you're the more materially successful partner, you need to cross that chasm, and in only one leap. This is how to start to do that. First, be very careful that you do not create a situation where your partner feels that she is keeping you from doing the kind of things that you love. That's what makes her feel that she will never have enough. Keep this in mind before you say, "Hey, let's go out to eat at this expensive restaurant," or "Let's go to Paris for the weekend," or "Let's go shopping at this exclusive store." Try just eating at home, or eat at places that she can afford to pay for as well. It is very important that you let her carry her own weight when it comes to money, otherwise before you know it she's going to feel powerless, which leads to feeling resentful.

Most of all, you need to examine your own heart. Ask yourself honestly, do you feel your partner is worth less because she makes less? Ask yourself, is there anything that you can do to help her make more? Ask yourself, what is true equality and where does it lie? In your bank book? In your bedroom? In your heart?

If I were giving *her* advice, I'd say this: Recognize that gifts of the heart are priceless. That your partner can buy anything that he wants for himself, but the only thing that he can't buy is love. Know that what you bring to this relationship that has true, everlasting value has nothing to do with money. You do, however, have to be strong and not overextend yourself financially just to keep up with him. You have to pay your own way when you can, and know when to draw the line when it comes to your partner spending money. Just because your partner may want to spend money and may have it to spend does not mean it's the best thing to do. Figure out how you can both equitably share the expenses as well as contribute to future investments. It is important not only to spend together but to save together, as I said in the answer before. Talk about this with each other, understand that it is hard, and know that sometimes when you accept less you are getting far more than all the money in the world can buy.

THE MONEY GRAB BAG

This section includes a variety of questions that don't fall under one single heading but seem to come up quite frequently. Browse through these questions—there's a good chance that you'll find one that, if you haven't wondered about it yet, you'll want to know the answer to sometime in the future.

I BLEW MY INHERITANCE—NOW WHAT?

Q. I recently lost my mother, and I received a lump sum of money from her retirement plan, which I have almost completely spent. I seem to fear keeping money, yet I also fear making it. Money just scares me, yet being without it is even worse.

A. Don't feel *too* bad—many, many people, at varying ages, have blown inheritances before you, and will in the future. When you think about it, not many of us have had much contact with a big lump sum of money. Yes, we deal with our monthly paycheck, which is usually spent as soon as we get it, and maybe we have a retirement account, which is locked up until we're 59.5 years of age. If we do encounter a lump sum it's usually either an inheritance or an early-retirement payoff from our place of employment.

Either way, when a sum of cash lands on our doorstep it is very scary and easy to blow. If this has happened to you and you wish you could at least get something out of the experience, carve how you feel about blowing it in your heart and in your mind. Vow to yourself that you will never blow any money again, not even just a little bit. If you make this vow and can keep to it, this will be one of the most valuable lessons you will ever have learned. So feel happy, rather than sad, that it happened.

The best advice financially I can give anyone who's afraid or anxious about having money is JUST DEAL WITH IT. Just start doing a few things to be responsible with your money. Once you do, you will see that it is far easier than you could have ever dreamed possible. So start right now to build up savings for yourself. It is never too soon to begin and it is never too late to start. Even if you think you do not have enough money to do this, you have to start putting as much as you can into a retirement account (see Step 4 in *The 9 Steps to Financial Freedom*). If you have a 401(k) or 403(b) at work, put the maximum that you can away. If not, open up an IRA now and start saving for your future. Let me show you why.

Let's say you put $2,000 a year in a retirement account every year from the age of twenty-five to thirty-four. After nine years of investing, age thirty-four, you go cuckoo and decide that you have had enough of this savings game, and are not going to put another cent into this account. While you're off doing you know what, this account continues to earn 8 percent year in and year out. When you're sixty-five and you need to live on the income from this money, how much will you have? Around 314,869 bucks. Not bad.

But watch: Let's say that you are now thirty-five years of age. And you have not put one cent away for retirement. But after a few looks in the mirror you somehow are hit with the fact that the forties and beyond are right around the corner and you'd better start saving for your retirement NOW, so you start putting that $2,000 a year away into a retirement account. And you do so for every year till you are sixty-five years of age. How much will you have when you are sixty-five? You might think since you have put $2,000 a year away for thirty years that you'd have a lot more than if you only put $2,000 a year away for nine years, wouldn't you? Wrong! You would have only $246,692.

So, even though you contributed $2,000 a year for twenty-two years longer, you have $68,177 less.

One more thing. In the first example, if you continue to put that $2,000 a year away every year till you are sixty-five, you will have $561,562—almost double what you would have if you waited till you were thirty-five to start. If you put as much as $4,000 a year away, you'll have over a million bucks. The key factor is not how much you save per year, it is when you started to save.

You cannot get back years no matter how hard you try—so my number-one tip for everyone reading this book is to *make every sacrifice you can to invest your money now.* The more you can put away starting right now, the better off you will be, and the less afraid you will become.

EARN MORE, SPEND MORE

Q. It seems as though every time I make some more money with a job change, I end up spending more than I was before. I just changed careers and got a little more income, only to find that somehow I now need a lot more! I haven't even taken a lavish trip to celebrate yet. The more I make, the further in debt I seem to get. What's going on?

A. Because it is one of the laws of money: *The more you make, the more you spend* (see page 122 of *The 9 Steps to Financial Freedom*). Most people spend every penny that comes home on their paycheck, regardless of how big the check is. Also, once you start making more, your mind automatically thinks it can spend more, so you start charging things and, guess what, when the bills come the money already has gone somewhere else. Sometimes a raise will put you in a higher tax bracket, and when all is said and done, after April 15 has come and gone, there really is not much, if any, left.

Because we think we are making more, we spend more, but in reality we end up with less! It really is crazy, but it is how it works. But there is a solution to this problem. The reverse of this money law is also true: *The less you think you make, the less you spend.* The key word here is *think.* You need to trick your mind into thinking that you make less than you actually do. The best way to do this is to start contributing the maximum that you can monthly to your retirement plan. When you do this—for instance via a 401(k) at work, where they take out a certain amount of money each and every paycheck before taxes to put into your retirement account—the paycheck that you bring home is smaller and therefore you end up spending less. Meanwhile, you are really saving more and more.

If you do not have a retirement plan at work that takes money out monthly, see if you can have your employer send a portion to a credit union for you so you never see it. This will have the same effect: your take-home check will not be as large and you'll spend less.

If this is not an option, you just have to be a little more disciplined and add to your bills yourself every paycheck period, meaning that the first person that you pay needs to be YOU. When you deposit your check, the first thing you should do is write a check directly payable to your IRA, SEP/IRA, or Keogh account. After you have made the maximum contribution for the year to these plans, keep taking the exact same amount of money and invest it in a good no-load mutual fund, again, so you will not be able to spend it. Pay yourself first, invest for yourself first, take care of your spending habits first—and you will soon see how you *can* make more and spend less.

REAL ESTATE

Q. Briefly explain capital gains tax and how it affects selling my house. How is it different before I'm fifty-five or after I'm fifty-five? I do not plan to buy another house.

A. It really is quite simple. Imagine that you bought your house for $60,000 and over the years you put $25,000 into the home to improve it. Your cost basis is the purchase price plus the cost of all improvements. In this example your cost basis would be $85,000 ($60,000 plus $25,000). Now let's say that today you have sold your house for $325,000 and have no plans to buy another home; you paid a 6 percent commission, or $19,500, to the real estate agent.

To figure what you'll owe capital gains tax on, take what you made from the sale ($325,000) and subtract from that your cost basis ($85,000) and also the cost to you of the sale ($19,500). In this case the amount you would owe capital gains tax on is $220,500 ($325,000 minus $19,500 minus $85,000). If you are under the age of fifty-five, you would owe a 28 percent capital gains tax on all $220,500, or $61,740, and there will be no way around that.

If you are fifty-five or older, however, you have a one-time-only exemption that could save you a considerable amount of money. It is known as the $125,000 exemption. After you reach age fifty-five, the government allows you a

$125,000 deduction from the capital gains on your home, as long as you have lived in your house as your primary residence for at least three out of the past five years. In this case, if you wanted to use the exemption, you would subtract $125,000 from the $220,500, leaving $95,500. This is the amount that you would owe that 28 percent capital gains tax on; if you did this, you would owe only $26,740, instead of $61,740. Using the $125,000 exemption will have saved you $35,000 in capital gains tax. (You see, there is one good thing about getting older!) Please note that the $125,000 can be used only once, and *only once per married couple.* If you happen to marry someone who has already used the $125,000 exemption on a home owned before you even knew him or her, you will not be able to use the exemption yourself. Yes, you read that correctly. Once you marry this person, the IRS will consider you one unit and deem that you married your exemption away. So if you own real estate and are thinking of getting married to someone over the age of fifty-five, it would be a good idea, before you get married, to ask if the exemption has been used. If he or she has used it, you should consider using your exemption before you're married.

Q. I am about to sell my home and buy another. Is there a way to avoid capital gains tax on this transaction?

A. Yes. Under certain circumstances you can roll or transfer your gains from home to home. In order to do this you

THE MONEY GRAB BAG

must buy or build a new home within two years of the sale of your old home, and the construction or purchase price of the new home must be equal to or more than the one you sold.

Let's put numbers to what I just said. To continue with the ones I used in the example above, your cost basis on your first home was $85,000. You sold this home for $325,000. Now suppose within two years you bought or built another home for $325,000 or more. Since you have met all the requirements, you could roll your cost basis of $85,000 from your old home into your new home and not have to pay any capital gains tax at all. In effect, you're deferring 100 percent of what you owed in capital gains taxes. As long as the transactions meet those requirements, there is no limit to the number of times you can do this.

Q. Does this mean if I buy another home, my new cost basis in the next home will be $325,000?

A. Now you are really dreaming. No, the $85,000 cost basis plus all improvements added on to it continue to roll with you.

So if on this second home that you bought for $325,000 you added $15,000 of improvements, that $15,000 will be added to the cost basis of $85,000 on the first home, giving you a new cost basis of $100,000. If you sell this second home for $500,000 and buy a new home for $500,000 or above, your cost basis is still $100,000. If you sell your third home a few years later and don't take the $125,000 exclusion and don't buy another home, you will owe capital gains tax on $400,000 ($500,000 minus $100,000).

Q. I live in a community-property state and the title of my house is in joint tenancy with my wife. I have been told that this is a big mistake, but this is how my realtor said to do it. You would think he would know. Is it a mistake or not?

A. Yes, it is a mistake. If you happen to live in Arizona, California, Idaho, Louisiana, Nevada, New Mexico, Texas, or Washington, and if you are married and jointly own any asset that has the potential to increase in value—such as a stock, or a piece of real estate—without a shadow of a doubt these assets should be held as *community property,* not joint tenancy. Let me compare joint tenancy to community property.

JOINT TENANCY

Suppose you and your wife bought a house as joint tenants for an original purchase price of $30,000. For tax purposes, your cost basis will be $15,000 and your wife's cost basis will also be $15,000. Now it is many years later and your wife has died. Because you owned the house in joint tenancy, her half of the house will pass to you immediately; no problem there. Also, since you have inherited her half of the house, so to speak, you will get a step up in the cost basis of her half. It will go from the original $15,000 to half the current value of the house when she died.

If the house was worth $300,000 when she died, her half is worth $150,000, and that becomes your new cost basis for the half of the property that you inherited from her. The cost basis on *your* half is still $15,000. To find the total cost basis for the house, you would add your original cost basis of $15,000 to the inherited cost basis of $150,000 for a total of $165,000. Let's say you now decide to sell this house for $300,000 and not buy another one, and you were not eligible to use the $125,000 exemption. You would owe income tax on $135,000 ($300,000 minus $165,000). That would be $37,800.

COMMUNITY PROPERTY

Everything is exactly the same up until the point that your wife dies. When you own something in community property, not only will you get a step up in cost basis on her half, *but you will get it on your half as well*. In this case, you each had a $15,000 cost basis. When your wife dies, her cost basis goes from $15,000 to $150,000 and so does yours. Your new cost basis for the house is not $165,000 as in joint tenancy, but $300,000. If you sell the house for $300,000 you'll owe nothing in income taxes.

As you can see, there is a big difference between owing $37,800 in taxes just because you held the title in joint tenancy and owing nothing because you held it in community property.

This concept holds true with any kind of investment, not just real estate. If you have a brokerage account or any investment on which you do not pay taxes till you sell it, that too should be held in community property. Assets that are not subject to capital gains, on which you pay taxes every year—such as bank accounts or money-market funds, Treasury notes, or CDs—can be held in joint tenancy, for there is no tax advantage to hold them in community property.

INVESTMENTS

Q. For the past ten years, every month I have put a sum of money into a mutual fund. Now I am ready to sell my shares. How do I know how much I will owe in taxes?

A. Since 1993, all mutual funds must report to you the average price per share that you bought the fund at. This is one easy way to determine the amount of gain or loss on this investment. However, you might want to figure out your results on a per-share basis. For instance, maybe you have some shares that you have a gain on and some that have a loss. You might want to sell those shares that you have a loss on to help you on your taxes, but keep the other shares to sell at a later date. If you used the average-price-per-share method that the mutual fund company will provide for you, you may on the average have a gain, which will not allow you to take full advantage of the shares that you have a loss in.

If this is of interest to you, you can figure out the cost per share on your own but it is complicated and time consuming. You have to keep track of the price you have paid for each share, from the very beginning. You also have to pay attention and record the dividends and capital gains that the fund distributes to you at the end of each year. Since dividends and short-term capital gains are reported to you as taxable income, if you reinvest these amounts to buy more shares, you must keep track of the cost of these shares as well. The total amount you have invested plus all reported taxable income that was reinvested through dividends and capital gains, subtracted from total sales proceeds received, will determine your taxable gain or loss.

Q. What does it mean to buy stocks on margin?

A. Buying on margin is essentially buying stocks with borrowed money. If you want to buy 100 shares of a stock that is selling for $50 a share, and if you have $5,000 in cash, you fork it over and you're the proud owner of those 100 shares. No one can take them from you till you decide to sell them. Suppose, however, you want to buy 100 shares of that stock but you *don't* have all $5,000. If you qualify, the brokerage firm that you are purchasing this stock from will lend you up to 50 percent of the amount you need to purchase the stock.

So if you had $4,000, you could borrow $1,000 from the brokerage firm and on paper own 100 shares of stock. This is known as buying stocks on margin. Why would the brokerage firm want to do this? Simple, since you are borrowing money from them, they are going to charge you interest. This interest is another source of income for them. Not only that, but they are going to hold the stock as collateral against this loan, so they have nothing to lose and everything to gain.

The danger for the investor comes in when the stock bought on margin happens to go down in price. By law, the brokerage firm can never let the collateral or the price of the stock fall below 50 percent of what they have lent. If the stock does go down that far, the firm issues what is known as a *margin call*—which means you, the investor, have to come up with some money right then and there. If you do not have the money, or cannot get it, the brokerage firm will sell the stock and take their money back and if there is any money left, then they give that back to the investor. On the other hand, if your stock happens to go up, you can do quite well, for you have made a profit on a greater number of shares than you would have without that leverage—as long as that additional profit is more than the interest cost you'll have to pay to the broker.

With any investment there is a trade-off between risk and reward. Buying on margin can increase your reward, but it also seriously increases your risk. When the stock that you are in goes up, margin can be great. But when you are on margin and the stock you are in goes down, you can be in big trouble. If your broker is encouraging you to buy on margin, you must keep in mind that the more shares of stock you buy, the more commission he will make, and that *the risk is all yours*. I personally would stay as far away from margin as possible, unless you consider yourself a sophisticated investor and are willing to take a big financial loss in pursuit of a possibly greater return.

PREPAID FUNERAL EXPENSES

Q. My mother, who is seventy, lives in Florida and has her burial plot in New York. She called and asked me if I thought it was wise for her to prepay her funeral expenses. She has been quoted a package which would send her body back to New York, pay for the chapel, the rabbi, and the cemetery fees, all for under $4,000. What should I tell her?

A. Well, my first words of advice would be simply to tell your mom NOT TO DIE! Look at some basic numbers: Actuarially speaking, she is likely to live another seventeen years. If she takes that $4,000 today and invests it in a good no-load mutual fund, which averages 10 percent return, in seventeen years that $4,000 will be worth $20,218. If you then discount back for inflation at 3 percent, that $20,218 would be worth $12,232 in today's dollars. So the question is, does your mom really want to spend over twelve thousand dollars to make sure everything is prepaid?

Equally important, buying this package leaves her no room to change her mind about her funeral arrangements. What if she meets a wonderful man in Florida, marries him, and later decides she would like to be buried with him? It could easily happen. What if she becomes a Buddhist and decides she would like a different sort of funeral?

If you think people don't make those changes at her age, you could be in for a big surprise. My mother, for instance, is eighty-two and, I must admit, is one hot mama for her age. (She's going to kill me for telling you all this.) For years she insisted she would be buried next to my dad, who passed away some time ago. Now, all of a sudden, she has been talking about how cremation makes more sense both emotionally and financially. I happen to agree with her, but this is something that she came to totally on her own. If she had prepaid her funeral expenses, not only would she have tied up money that could have been invested elsewhere, but she would have been locked into something that she seems not to want to do anymore. So the short answer to your question (now that I have given you the long one) is, I think prepaid funerals are a waste of money.

TREASURIES INFLATION PROTECTION
SECURITIES

Q. I heard on TV last summer that the U.S. government would market savings bonds at the first of the year that would earn 4 percent above the CPI, so they would automatically beat inflation. Have you heard of these?

A. The bonds you are talking about will be available in 1997, and they're called TIPS—Treasuries Inflation Protection Securities. They will have maturities of ten years and will be available in minimum denominations of $1,000. They will be sold in the same way that regular Treasuries are sold and that is with a quarterly auction. To buy them directly, call 202-874-4000 to find out where the nearest branch of the Federal Reserve is to you and/or to set up a Treasury Direct account to purchase them through the mail. Also there will be a TIPS mutual fund available through American Century (800-345-2021) as well as PIMCO and MFS. The minimum to open the account will be $2,500. Sometime soon you will also see them popping up in your 401(k)s, and you will also be able to get them through payroll deductions for as little as $50.

You should know that these bonds work a little differently from the way you described in your question. The interest rate on the bond doesn't float; it remains constant. However, the value of the bond is recalculated regularly depending on the inflation rate. Here's what I mean: The first batch of TIPS that comes out is expected to be priced at a yield of around 3.38 percent. That means that if you invested $1,000 and there was no inflation that year, you would get $33.75 in interest, or $16.88 every six months (since these bonds pay interest every six months). But let's say there's inflation and that after six months, the CPI climbs 1 percent. Now they will reprice the bond by that 1 percent—so the value of your bond would now be $1,010, rather than the $1,000 that you paid. Now that the bond is worth more, the 3.38 percent in interest, which is fixed for the whole ten years, would be also paid out on that new value. So rather than getting $16.88 for that six months, you would get $17.04 for that payment. If the CPI climbs another 2 percent, for example, they will reprice your bond to $1,030 and your next interest payment will be $17.38. They will do this every six months.

Keep in mind that when the price of your bonds is adjusted upward, you'll owe tax on that money that year if you hold these outside of a retirement account. Even though you will not get that money till you sell or the bond matures, you will still have to pay tax on it—so it is possible that you will owe more in taxes than you got in income. The bonds are geared at people who want protection against inflation more than they want current income, and are best suited to be held in a retirement account.

INDEX

AB trusts, 22
attorney in fact, 35, 36
  more than one, 37–38, 39
  trust in, 40

bank accounts:
  marriage and, 103–4
  payable-on-death (POD), 23–24, 26
bankruptcy, 85, 91–93
beneficiaries, 23–26
  estates as, 24
  payable-on-death accounts and,
    23–24, 26
  taxes and, 25, 26, 28
  trusts as, 25–26

capital-gains taxes, 32, 33, 113–16,
    118
COBRA, 66–67
collection agencies, 87–89
college financial aid, 73
  divorce and, 79–80
  finding information on, 80
  residency and, 76–77
  and uniform gift to minors
    accounts, 76
college tuition, 73–76
  investing for, 73, 75, 77–79
  prepaid plans, 73–74
  and uniform gift to minors
    accounts, 74–76
community property, 90–91, 116,
    117–18
credit cards, 80–85, 89–91
  applying for, 81
  bankruptcy and, 92–93
  credit limits of, 94
  fees of, 94, 95–96
  interest rates on, 81, 83–85, 86,
    94–95
  investing with cash advances from,
    81–82
  monthly payments on, 84–85
  paying off, investing and, 83
  secured, 87
  of spouse, 90–91, 103–4
  what to look for in, 93–95
  withdrawing IRA funds to pay off,
    89–90
  see also debt

credit reports, 85–86
credit shelter trusts, 22
custodial care, 53, 55

debt, 80–96
  bankruptcy and, 85, 91–93
  collection agencies and, 87–89
  credit reports and, 85–86
  investing borrowed money, 81–82
  spouse's spending habits and, 97–99
  see also credit cards
dental insurance, COBRA and, 66–67
divorce:
  college financial aid and, 79–80
  wills and, 10
durable power of attorney, 19, 36–42
  accounting of, 39
  attorney in, 35, 36, 37–38, 39, 40
  cost of, 41
  granting to more than one person,
    37–38, 39
  laws regarding, 41–42
  power of attorney vs., 35–36
  refusal to honor, 38
  revocation of, 36–37

estates, 29
  as beneficiaries, 24
  taxes and, 22, 28, 29, 30, 33
  see also beneficiaries; gifting;
    revocable living trusts; wills

Fair Debt Collection Practices Act,
    88–89
financial aid, see college financial aid
401(k) plans, 109, 112
  rolling over into IRAs, 67–68, 70,
    72
  taxes and, 69–70, 71
  withdrawing funds from, 69–70, 71
funeral expenses, prepaid, 121–22

gifting, 27–34
  taxes and, 27, 28, 30–33, 43–44
  and transferring assets in order to
    qualify for Medicaid, 42–44,
    50–52
  uniform gift to minors accounts,
    74–76
grants, 80

125

INDEX

A FINAL WORD

So that just about does it. I hope this book serves as a quick reference guide for you and helps to answer your questions. If you need more detailed information about some of the topics covered here, you will be able to find what you are looking for in my other two books, *You've Earned It, Don't Lose It* and *The 9 Steps to Financial Freedom*. If you still have a question that needs answering, please feel free to write to me. I will write back to you personally to see in what way I can help you. Remember, all you have to do is *Ask Suze*.

Please write:

Suze Orman
2000 Powell Street, Suite 1605
Emeryville, CA 94608